CW00735473

Library Classification

C.K. Sharma
Amit K. Sharma

ATLANTIC
PUBLISHERS & DISTRIBUTORS (P) LTD

Published by

ATLANTIC

PUBLISHERS & DISTRIBUTORS (P) LTD

B-2, Vishal Enclave, Opp. Rajouri Garden,
New Delhi-110027
Phones : 25413460, 25429987, 25466842

Sales Office
7/22, Ansari Road, Darya Ganj,
New Delhi-110002
Phones : 23273880, 23275880, 23280451
Fax : 91-11-23285873
web : www.atlanticbooks.com
e-mail : info@atlanticbooks.com

Printed in India
at Nice Printing Press, Delhi

Preface

Classification is an artificial arrangement of documents or likewise. We classify the things whether in home, shops or the library. It needs a system based on normative principles. There are many systems of classification in practice at national and international level, like DDC and CC, UDC, LC and other schemes. All have their fundamental principles. However, there are a few canons, principles and laws which evaluate a scheme of classification.

This book studies the basic factors of library classification which are logical and scientific. It will prove useful to students of Library and Information Science. Besides, for the library professionals this will serve as a useful manual.

In completing this task, I received ardent support from my wife Smt. Indira Sharma who has always encouraged me to contribute something more to the field of Library and Information Science. I am thankful to her for all the encouragement and unstinting support.

I am also grateful to Dr. K.R. Gupta, Chairman, M/s Atlantic Publishers & Distributors (P) Ltd., New Delhi, for publishing this book in a record time.

C.K. SHARMA

Contents

Classifying a Thing – A Basic Factor

1. Senses. There are many senses which are used for knowing something. In addition to senses, there are other factors which work, i.e. reason, memory, intuition, etc.

2. Relationship. It is another stage of classification. It includes:

(a) Group of ideas.

(b) Group of subjects in helpful sequence.

3. Practice is based on theory. The first step is theory which is experimented and turned to practical process.

4. Ancient phase. In ancient period also there was a sense of classification. It is known as Vedic Classification. It was based on:

(a) *Dharma* (Religion): According to religions.

(b) *Artha* (Economy): When we go through Kautilya's *Arthashastra*, we find many economic aspects which were considered the stages of classification.

(c) *Kama* (Work): Kama means work, activities, process which have many aspects and these aspects were considered as stages of classification.

(d) *Moksha* (Salvation): The last breath, last stage and the end part of any work is a stage which was considered for classification.

5. Greek civilization. It is called utility based classification. All psychological aspects were considered in the period:

(a) *Theoretical Philosophy*: It is one of the aspects of Greek civilization, i.e. Logic, Metaphysics, Maths and Physics.

(b) *Practical Philosophy*: It is a practical aspect of Philosophical theory. It is classified in three aspects: Ethics, Political Science and Economics.

(c) *Fine Art*: It is also known as Productive art. It is classified in two aspects, i.e. Applied Science and useful art.

Greek classification is an ancient classification and based on fundamentals.

6. Baconian classification. This classification was evolved by Francis Bacon (1561-1626).

Class I — Historical aspects (History and Geography)

Class II — Poetry (Arts and Literature)

Class III — Philosophy which is based on reason.

(a) *Science of God*

(b) *Science of Nature*

    (i) Primary philosophy

    (ii) Physics

    (iii) Meteaphysics

    (iv) Magic (Astronomy)

    (v) Natural Philosophy.

(c) *Science of Man*

7. Camte's classification. It was evolved by August Camte (1798-1857).

8. Spenser's classification. It was evolved by Hercort Spenser, (1820-1930).

1.1 Knowledge

Knowledge means the whole universe. In other words, know + ledge means to know about something. Man being a human being has three specific characteristics: (a) Intellect (b) Wisdom (c) Mind. Man thinks with no check and conserves it in his mind. Mind is a reservoir in which intellect work rests with liberty. Knowledge should not be checked or move abrupt. It should flow freely from one mind to the other. All these three characteristics are the creation of man. When the men apply intellect with wisdom and preserve and retrieve through mind, it is called idea or thinking. Thinking is a continuous process of development based on experience and observation. It has resulted into knowledge explosion.

Dr. S.R. Ranganathan has suggested three ways of knowledge explosion:

(a) Idea plane,

(b) Verbal plane,

(c) Notational plane.

Idea plane denotes thinking and keeping in mind what is not verbal or notational. Every man thinks, creates ideas in his mind. This is called Idea plane.

Verbal plane denotes the ideas which are spoken verbally. Man has many ideas in his mind based on his experience and observation and stores them in his mind. But when he expresses the ideas in language or through other expression media, it is called verbal plane.

Notational plane leads to notations. When ideas come in mind and converted into language and take verbal shape and the verbal language is converted into artificial language in coding in any form of notations, i.e. alphabets, Arabic numeric, signs and symbols and/or Greek letters, such coding is known as notational plane.

Attributes of Knowledge

(a) **Spiral of development of new subjects**: Relay research leading to a spiral movement for short period in the development of new subjects:

(i) Fundamental research: Research in pure science.

(ii) Applied research: Specific field of utility.

(iii) Pilot project: Establishment of production of commodity. The spiral continues and thus emerge new subjects.

(b) **Continuum:** Universe of knowledge is continuum. Subject grows and leads in decreasing degree of interaction—Extension and intension between it and other subjects. It leads to mutual enrichment of the subjects and it is a development of new specialisation.

(c) **Infinite:** Universe of subjects are continuously grows with the increase in facilities. Infinite means impossible to measure or without limit. With the continuous knowledge explosion, subjects grow without limit which is impossible to measure.

(d) **Multidimensional/manifold multidimensional:** Knowledge grows in manifold dimensions, witnessing exponential rate among the classes of knowledge, e.g. arrays of classes, collateral arrays, chain of classes, etc.

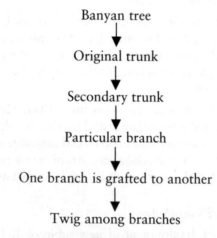

Banyan tree

↓

Original trunk

↓

Secondary trunk

↓

Particular branch

↓

One branch is grafted to another

↓

Twig among branches

Similarly tree of knowledge grows in three dimensions.

(e) **Turbulently Dynamic:** It is an important attribute. There are two types of ideas—seminal and near seminal ideas. These are increasing through centuries.

Turbulent means circles of universe of knowledge. Relay-research is producing micro-subjects continuously.

Example: 225 lacs periodicals   - every year

70,000 new titles   - every year

15 million pieces of information   - every year

There is no end to it. More scientific papers are poured like rain over the scientific world used in a year.

Man has mind, mind has ideas and ideas are subjects. Man gains knowledge in three phases:

(a) Man and Nature— Natural Science.

(b) Man and Self-Humanities.

(c) Man and Society— Social Science.

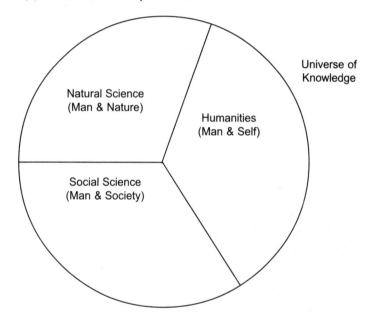

In fact the classification of work started the day the men started naming the things.

In Rome, the word class is used for the "class and persons of the society" and the word classification is supposed to be originated from classic.

1.1.1 Knowledge Classification

The universe of knowledge consists of an infinite number of

entities which are now unknown. Those which are unknown will become known in future.

Therefore, a scheme of classification should have Infinite hospitality to accommodate newly known entities in array and chains.

Special features:

Knowledge classification is a basis of Book Classification.

Classification starts with knowledge. If there is no knowledge, there is no classification.

All knowledge could be systematically mapped out according to the recognised rules of division to form a complete classification of ideas.

There is a true order of the science.

It is a philosophical basis for library classification.

It is followed by intellectual climate and evolutionary order or order of nature. It is an order of progression from simple to complex things.

Knowledge classification is considered as over. As a theoretical approach, it is:

(a) Relatively broad.

(b) Neglecting principles of subject analysis.

(c) Order of nature is restricted field.

(d) Not a practical approach.

Documents:

(a) It is a record of work on paper or other material.

(b) It is fit for physical handling.

(c) It is transportable.

(d) It can be preserved through time.

Type:

(a) Handwritten; (b) Printed; (c) Typed; (d) Means of communication (sound recording, photographic production).

Kinds:

(a) Books; (b) Periodicals; (c) Maps; (d) Sound recording; (e) Others.

1.1.2 Document (Book) Classification

When the knowledge takes the shape of a document, it involves certain additional features not found in the Universe of Knowledge. These drive from the subtle and gross embodiments involved in a book and from readers service, in order to fulfil the laws of Library Science. Additional features are:

(a) Quasi class: The class which is specific in nature.

(b) Local variations: Based on local problems.

(c) Composite documents: Documents which have complex nature.

(d) Partial comprehension.

(e) Form or medium of expression: Medium which is used for expression.

(f) Related documents: Documents which are based on likeness.

(g) Physique of the documents: Physical body of the document.

Ranganathan enunciated these parts of document classification:

(i) Book number
(ii) Collection number
(iii) Distinctiveness

These are also called Canons. These are the additional canons.

Special features:

1. It is a structural organisation of knowledge.

2. It is well-constructed.

3. It will serve with maximum efficiency of functional organisation of knowledge.

4. It consists of grouping and sub-grouping of subjects.

5. Grouping is based on experience and further requirements.

6. It is well-qualified to serve.

7. It is established in the scientific and educational concerns.

    8. It leads to efficiency.

    9. It leads to adequacy.

  10. It leads to educational value.

  11. It is a practical classification.

  12. It is a purposeful classification.

Limitations of Book Classification:

(a) Its purpose is to arrange books and other materials in helpful order. It depends on careful consideration of possible facet formula within each subject.

(b) No helpful order can satisfy fully.

(c) The passage of time leads radical changes of classification scheme. Tremendous labour is required to meet the challenge of enormous increasing record.

(d) Even the best book classification is unable to bring together all the material on the shelves. Books can be scattered according to their nature.

(e) Interdiscipline researches have put a problem before the classifier to keep books of just similar thoughts together.

(f) Poor and faulty work of the classifier in difficult and unfamiliar fields.

(g) Inaccurate and makeshift decisions due to poorly constructed and outdated table of classification.

(h) Long and confusing notation for specific subjects.

(i) It is effective for one language only.

1.1.3 Difference between Knowledge and Book Classification

Knowledge Classification	Book Classification
1. It arranges knowledge on the basis of evaluating and classified thoughts, ideas and concepts for universal purpose.	It arranges expression of the knowledge.
2. It represents adequately the field of human learning.	Expression preserved in written records,

3. It is based on preconceived ideas, essentially superficial.

documents with specific purpose.

It provides adequate subject approach to the existing collection.

4. It is based on personal theories and a new doctrine might upset.

It is based on systems and principles and new doctrines facilitate the way of book classification.

5. Knowledge classification is multidimensional.

It has to be one dimensional from left to right along the shelf.

6. Reality cannot be classified, only our knowledge of it exists as expressed thoughts.

It is a convenient device for location of known works.

7. The terms which are unlinear, must be set down before classification can be made.

Book classification can be constructed by producing helpful arrangement and based on the 'order of nature'.

8. It is mental planning of the thought (subject).

It is a transcribing of thoughts in subjects.

9. It consists of main branch of universe of knowledge.

It consists of terms of the knowledge.

10. It is human mental faculty.

It contains words and phrases used for human mental faculties.

11. It is a homogeneous region of the universe of knowledge.

It is a first array of schemes and each term of array makes a great area of knowledge.

1.1.4 Classification

It is a result of the arrangement of various classes.

= Putting similar entities together.

= Separating unlike entities.

= The features, qualities, attributes of the entities may be similar among themselves or may be different from one another.

Similar: Economics, Commerce, Pol. Science, Sociology

Sanskrit — Hindi, Philosophy.

Different: Economics → Philosophy.

Sanskrit → Commerce.

— Classification is used for grouping of facts.

— The purpose of grouping may be general or special.

Kinds of Classification:

(a) Natural Classification (Knowledge classification).

(b) Artificial Classification (Book classification).

1.1.5 Natural Classification and Artificial Classification

Natural Classification	Artificial Classification
1. Classification based on important points of similarity.	Classification according to some unimportant or less important points of resemblance.
2. It is grouping of thesis according to nature's plan and order.	Grouping of things according to the purpose of individual concerned.
3. It is an objective classification.	It is subjective classification.
4. It is for general purpose.	It is for specific purpose.
5. Natural classification is a language of ideas, mind and thoughts.	Book classification is a language of ordinal numbers.
6. It is expressed through methods of expression, not merely through words.	It is expressed through words, Finger language, Cyber language.
7. It is designed for extensive thoughts and knowledge.	It is designed for specific purpose of mechanising arrangement.

Both classifications are presumptions of man, both are similar. It is very difficult to point out similarity and unsimilarity.

DEFINITIONS OF CLASSIFICATION

Classification

J. Farradans: "Classification is a theory of the structure of knowledge and the principles of classification must, therefore, be based on an adequate understanding of the nature of knowledge. Classification is not some part of 'an external reality' wanting to be discovered; it is an intellectual upon mental entities or concepts."

W.C. Berwick Sayers: "The arrangement of books on shelves or description accounts them in the manner which is most useful to those who read."

Margaret Mann: "Classification is the arranging of things according to likeness and unlikeness. It is the sorting and grouping of things, but in addition, classification of books is a knowledge classification with adjustments made necessary in the physical form of books."

S.R. Ranganathan: "It is a translation of the name of the subject of a book into preferred artificial language of ordinal numbers, and the individualisation of several books dealing with the same specific subject by means of further set of ordinal numbers which represent some features of the book other than their thought contents."

Therefore, classification is a process by which we can group things according to their likeness and unlikeness and separate them according to their attributes. This process is automatic. Classification is primarily a mental process because we group things in an order according to concepts or ideas in our mind. J.S. Mill says that the purpose of classification is primarily "to facilitate the operations of the mind in clearly conceiving and retaining in memory the character of the objects in question". Five laws of library science are satisfied by the standard scheme of classification. If classification scheme is proper, all books will be used, every reader will get his book, every book finds its readers, it saves the time of the reader and this will result the growth of the library providing maximum service to the readers. Dr. Ranganathan says that proper arrangement of books on shelves will solve all problems of library service. More collection does not warrant any effective use. Proper steps for systematic orderly arrangement and means of revelation or making the sources of the library known to its reader are essential.

The users of the library are the guests and the librarian is their host, though from experience it is found that something else is needed other than personal assistance. It is material/ documents and their arrangements. Arrangement should be made in such a way that it displays resources of the library with maximum clarity and any given item can promptly be located.

There are many possible ways of arranging books, either by size, colour of binding, press, publisher, date of publication, title, author, subject or by accession register number. However, documents may be arranged by:

(a) Type of books: Children books, rare books, etc.

(b) Nature of books: Fiction, literature, etc.

(c) Physical features: Binding, bound periodicals, phonorecords.

(d) Size.

(e) Subjects.

Subject arrangement is thought to be the best arrangement of documents. It is most necessary for the maximum utilisation of resources of the library. Many readers do, of course, link their readings with a particular subject but most of the readers consult their books under subject and need subject approach while consulting the library. In special libraries the most common approach is subject approach. The user generally wants to know if the literature available on a library material is essential. Readers requiring books by author and title should also be served nicely.

Classification of subjects divides a collection into small groups on the basis of likeness and unlikeness so that reader can pick up his book easily. Subject will have to be basis for classifying books and other library material. In classification, when we use the term subject, we always mean specific subject. For example a book on public library will go under public library, not under library science. Berwick Sayers says, "To classify accurately and precisely, we must place each book in specific subject. Within each major subject field, the sequence should begin with general material and proceed slowly to more specialised branches of subject." The specific subject of a book is determined by examining the thought contents and translated to ordinal numbers according to a scheme of classification.

Helpful Order: Classification brings related subjects together and thus gives a helpful sequence to the books on the shelves. The purpose of classification is to arrange books in a helpful order. It also helps to mechanise the correct replacing of books returned after use. A classification is applied in libraries. It brings like books together. It saves time in finding them. It reveals the weakness or strength of the collection. Classification also helps user in making sure that they always know the order or sequence of subjects.

Alphabetical Arrangement: Classified arrangement is the best arrangement for serious reading or for reference service and for information retrieval. Alphabetical arrangement cannot be completely rejected. Alphabetical order is used within a classification scheme wherever it can bring about a more useful grouping than a classified sequence. Whenever necessary, alphabetical order may be used by subject, or by author or by title.

2

Concept of Subject Approach

Bliss's views: There are indeed two kinds of classification: On one hand—logical, natural, scientific, on the other hand—the practical, the arbitrary, the purposive.

It can be expressed in the following way:

Classification	Division
1. Consists in grouping individual items —	Division in reverse process—
(i) Grouping in classes.	(i) Dividing classes and further sub-classes.
2. We proceed from less general to more general or from smaller extension to greater extension.	We proceed from more general to less general or from greater extension to smaller extension.
3. It is inductive.	It is deductive.

Ranganathan stressed on subject approach and likeness and unlikeness :

   (a) Subject approach based on likeness and unlikeness.

   (b) More minute classification, more helpful.

Palmer and Wells :

Reader's first choice is subject approach.

Knowledge is embodied in documents.

Documents are the subjects of universe of knowledge.

Subject approach is effected by:

(a) Individualisation of documents.

(b) Grouping of like documents.

Mills explains the aspects influencing the library to have separate sequence:

(a) Age of reader.

(b) Grade of reader.

(c) Current stock.

(d) Reserve stock.

(e) Size of documents.

(f) Physical fitness of documents.

(g) Factual literature.

(h) Imaginary literature.

(i) Language of document.

(j) Document of temporary significance.

(k) Value of documents — rare material.

(l) Form of document — bound periodical.

(m) Date of printing.

(n) Textbooks.

(o) Document to different sexes.

(p) Document for abnormal readers—blinds.

Specific Subject: We can divide such subjects in three categories:

(a) Simple specific subject— Main subject 'Psychology'.

(b) Compound specific subject—First order of main subject.

Example: Feelings in abnormal psychology: Psychology —Abnormal Psychology.

Complex specific subject: Second or more order of main subject.

Example: Feeling in abnormal psychology in relation to social customs.

Psychology: Abnormal Psychology + Sociology.

Ranganathan has further classified the subjects on the basis of three planes:

(a) Idea plane: It is product of thinking, reflecting, imagining, by aid to logic, intuition and ideas deposited in the memory.

(b) Verbal plane: Which is a spoken stage of subject/class.

(c) Notational plane: Which is a stage of coding.

Idea Plane	Verbal Plane	Notational Plane
Class	Subject	Class number
Isolate idea	Isolate term	Isolate number
Facet idea	Facet term	Facet number
Basic class	Basic subject	Basic class number
Main class	Main subject	Main class number
Canonical class	Canonical subject	Canonical class number
Idea	Term	Number

Notational plane is represented by:

(i)   Arabic numerals   1,2,3,......8,9,0

(ii) Roman capitals   ABCD.....XYZ

(iii) Roman small   a b, c......x, y, z

(iv) Greek alphabets $\alpha \infty$

(v)   Punctuation marks   , ; : . !

This is artificial language called classificatory language.

2.1 Purpose of Classification

1. To separate subjects on the basis of likeness and unlikeness.

2. To make grouping and sub-grouping of subjects.

3. To arrange things in the most convenient order.

Example: Garment shop: Garments are arranged by the market trends.

Grocer's shop: Commodities are arranged in different ways so that the grocer can go straight to the shelves containing sugar, tea, etc.

4. To make the books available to every reader.

5. To enable the reader to receive his book.

6. To arrange the books in classified order.

7. To retrieve the information whenever needed.

8. To make available the whole library stock to readers by publisher, date of publication, title, by author or by subjects. The proper way is to arrange by contents of the material.

2.2 Functions of Classification

Sayers: Books are foundation of library. Classification is a foundation of librarianship.

There are following functions of classification :

1. Arranges books and other material in helpful sequence.

2. Ensures speedy location.

3. Replacement of books for next user.

4. Provides reader's approach to subsidiary subjects by analysing entries in the classified catalogue.

5. Reveals the strength and weakness of the stock of books.

6. Enables the librarian to built up a balanced collection.

7. Helps the systematic arrangement.

8. Helps the librarian to put new books with the related books when added in library.

9. Individualises each subject within its relevant class.

10. Provides means by which the stock of the books and other material may be clearly and effectively guided.

11. Facilitates display of books/documents and withdrawal of certain books from the main stock.

12. Makes up his collection for different centres or branches.

13. Helps in stock verification by self list.

14. Helps the librarian to recover the cost of books.

15. Facilitates the compilation of various kinds of statistics and reflects the demands on various sections of the stock.

16. It is a basis of recording issue books in lending counter.
17. Helps in compilation of bibliographies, categories.
18. Facilitates the systematic filing of correspondence.
19. It is a time-saving device.
20. It is a mechanical device.
21. Helps to provide "the right book to the right man and fulfil the law "Every book finds its readers".

2.3 Limitations of Classifications

1. The size of the book, resulting in the need for proper sequence on the shelves.
2. Complexity of knowledge, as recorded in the book.
3. Long notations (Colon and D.C., UDC).
4. Difficult to classifying special material or non-book material.
5. Keeping the scheme up-to-date without introducing radical changes.

All these factors make its effectiveness.

2.4 Principles of Classification

Rechardson says:

(a) The books are collected for use.
(b) Books are administered for use.
(c) Books are arranged for use.

1. **Subject Approach:** If classification helps in use of books, a method of systematic arrangement is adopted, though it is logical or not. The subject arrangement of the documents is found suitable for both readers and librarians, but it is also necessary to arrange the books on the basis of thought contents.

Library classification is classification of knowledge (thought contents). Hence, schemes of classification emerged to classify books according to their thought contents.

2. **Porphyry's Tree:** Knowledge is totality, and classification starts from knowledge. It is like a porphyry tree (Greek logic) in which a species is derived from genus of the discovery of

difference, so the genus is shown to divide into two species, one of which possesses the difference and the other does not. Only two classes would appear at each stage. This division is known as dichotomous division since only two classes are distinguished. D.C. and L.C. rejected it as they started with large subject and divided them up.

The value of Porphyry's tree is that:

(i) Classification leads the coordinate classes based on the principle of division.

(ii) There is a presentation of subject on the basis of thought contents, i.e. quality.

3. **Extension and Intention:** It is logical that in a general classification designed to cover all departments of knowledge, a collection of books will be broken up into organised subjects group using one characteristic at a time.

The characteristics used in division enable to assemble things according to their degree of likeness to make a specific class.

Classification proceeds from terms of great extension (denotation) and small intension (connotation).

Each class is a species of one immediately above it in hierarchical chain and a genus in relation to the above. This principle is followed at each stage while dividing a class.

4. **Inductive and Deductive Nature of Classification:** The main problem in classification is to classify the subjects. All subjects share or involve attributes that make them member of a class.

Example: Mathematics-Arithmetic-Algebra-Geometry-Trigonometry.

It shows that classification is an inductive one, which builds broader classes from narrower classes, working from the particular to the general. But in practice, library classifications are usually constructed of the opposite process of division working deductive from the general to specific. In other words, classification of subject is known as classification of documents.

5. **Aristotelian Pattern**: Aristotle has given an account of logical classification. This is based on logic.

Most of the classification schemes have a structure of logical classification of Aristotelian pattern, i.e. division of classes—general to specific. Sub-species by the addition of one different characteristics after another.

Aristotelian pattern: Division was dichotomous at each step, i.e. each genus was divided into two groups—A and Not A. One possessing the characteristics and the other not.

A subject of a book should determine its order if it is to be helpful. It enables the reader to consult all books at one place relating to one subject or other related subjects together. In short, like books should be brought together so that they may be used in relation to one another. This means subjects should be arranged according to their degree of relation.

6. **Hierarchical Structure of Classification**: Hierarchical concept is based on the assumption that the process of subdivision must exhibit as much as possible the natural hierarchy of the subject, proceeding from greater extension and small intention to those of smaller extension and greater intention.

Bliss says: General work first followed by work on general subjects treated especially, than by works on special subject treated generally, and lastly by works on special subjects treated specially.

Example:

   (i) The general treated generally — Locomotive.

  (ii) The general treated specially — Loco-design.

 (iii) The special treated generally — Electric Locomotive.

 (iv) The special treated specially — Electric Loco-design.

2.5 Principles of Division

Shera and Egan have given the following account of the principle of a hierarchy:

   (a) The hierarchical proceeds by the assembly of the groups of sciences of the principal fields of knowledge into main classes of divisions. Such classes have great extension and small intention.

(b) The process is based on different qualities of which each main class, and thus sub-classes or sub-divisions are made.

(c) Each sub-division in three classes is divided by further different values to produce still further sub-divisions and more sections and sub-sections and likewise process continues.

(d) Each single set of sub-divisions may consist of classes of equal ranks, a coordinate position.

Order of subject in array: (Ranganathan)

(a) Canonical order: Traditional and conventional sequence.

(b) Evolutionary order: If same line of evolution, earlier is first.

(c) Spatial contiguity: Geographical area.

(d) Chronological order: If two classes belong to an earlier point of time, then one must have precedence over other.

(e) Alphabetical order.

(f) Increasing complexity: If one class deals with lesser degree of complexity than the other, then that must have precedence over the other.

(g) Consistent order: Consistency should be maintained.

3

Canons

Canons are the foundation of library classification. Canons provide a scientific basis.

They serve as:

- (a) Guidelines for classificationists /classifier.
- (b) Touchstone to assess the efficiency in the scheme of classification.

First edition of *Prolegomena to Library Classification* (1937) included integrated theory:

- (a) Mainly descriptive.
- (b) Practices prevalent at the time.

Ranganathan provided largest list of principles (canons). He divided the theory of classification into three parts:

- (a) General theory of classification.
- (b) Theory of knowledge classification.
- (c) Theory of document classification.

3.1 General Theory of Classification

It evolves more in three planes:

- (a) **Idea Plane**: It involves six inherent concepts:
  - (i) Characteristics.
  - (ii) Succession of characteristics.
  - (iii) Arrays of classes.
  - (iv) Chain of classes.

    (v) Filiatory sequence.

    (vi) Additional canons.

Every concept has five sets of canons in the idea plane.

   (i) Canon of characteristics-4.

  (ii) Canon of succession of characteristics-3.

 (iii) Canon of array-4.

 (iv) Canon of chain-2.

  (v) Canon of filiatory sequence-2.

There are also two additional canons :

    (a) Terminology.

    (b) Notation.

 (b) **Verbal plane**—It has 4 canons.

 (c) **Notation plane**—First set has 2 canons.

    Second set has 5 pairs of canons.

3.2 Theory of Knowledge Classification

Universe of knowledge has infinite number of entities, some are known and some unknown.

It has three concepts:

 (a) Hospitality in array — 2 canons.

 (b) Hospitality in chain — 2 canons.

 (c) Mnemonics — 5 canons.

Notations have an important role.

Notation system satisfies these nine canons, in addition to canons of general theory of classification.

3.3 Theory of Document Classification

When knowledge takes the shape of a document, it involves additional features, which are not found in the universe of knowledge.

Features:

 (a) Quasi-class.

 (b) Local variation.

 (c) Composite document.

(d) Partial comprehensive.

(e) Form or medium of expression.

(f) Related documents.

(g) Physique of the documents.

There are three additional canons in the theory of document classification.

(i) Canon of book number.

(ii) Canon of collection number.

(iii) Canon of distinctiveness.

3.3.1 Canon of Characteristics (Idea Plane)

$$\left.\begin{array}{l}\text{A thing} \\ \text{A concept} \\ \text{An idea}\end{array}\right\rbrace \text{is a quality} \longrightarrow \left.\begin{array}{l}\text{quality of entity} \\ \text{property of entity}\end{array}\right\rbrace \begin{array}{l}\text{is called} \\ \text{'attribute'.}\end{array}$$

An entity may have various attributes.

Basis of Classification: It has two aspects—

(a) Grouping like entities.

(b) Separating unlike entities.

Attributes based on characteristics: Only those attributes which fulfil certain conditions are used as basis of classification. Such attributes are named as characteristics.

Hence, canons which concern the characteristics chosen for classification are called "Canon of Characteristics".

A characteristic used to classify a universe should satisfy the following four canons:

(a) Canon of differentiation (applicable to universe of basic subject).

(b) Canon of relevance (applicable to universe of isolate idea).

(c) Canon of ascertainability (applicable to universe of compound subjects).

(d) Canon of performance (applicable to universe of complex subjects).

3.3.1.1 Canon of Differentiation

Entities are divided in classes and each class is differentiated on the basis of characteristics.

Example: Large group of students into small groups. On the basis of sex, height, weight, mother tongue and marks.

3.3.1.2 Canon of Relevence

Classification divides the universe of books into convenient groups to suit the requirements of readers in the library—subject matter, language, author, year of publications, etc. These are relevant characteristics.

3.3.1.3 Canon of Ascertainability

Sometimes relevant characteristics are not ascertainable and definite. Date of birth is ascertainable characteristics. In 14th ed. D.C. in European literature, writers are divided as major writers and minor writers. But it is difficult to ascertain who is major and who is minor. Today major writer may be minor by tomorrow. Today minor writer may be major writer by tomorrow. This violation of this canon has been removed in 18th ed. In C.C. this canon is fully followed. Every writer is given due importance.

3.3.1.4 Canon of Permanence

This canon means that there are some characteristics of entities which are not changed, and are used for likeness and unlikeness.

It has been the tradition to divide periodicals into two classes, namely:

(i) Periodicals published by learned societies.

(ii) Periodicals not published by learned societies.

It is difficult to divide such societies. Height, weight, mother tongue are permanent characteristics. But hair style, colour of sari are not permanent characteristics and hence classification cannot be perfect.

Sponsoring body of periodical also changes with the change of name of periodical. However, subject never changes. Hence, it is a permanent characteristic.

3.4 Canon for Succession of Characteristics

It has three concepts.

3.4.1 Canon of Concomitance

'Concomitance' means concurrence or agreement. This canon should not be used in succession for classifying a universe into different classes, because they give rise to one and the same result.

Example: Age and year of birth should not be used in succession for classifying a group of boys into different classes for they will give rise to the same set of classes.

No two character should be concomitant, i.e. giving the same sequence. If we arrange by date of birth, the same sequence will be there.

3.4.2 Canon of Relevant Succession

Literature has four characteristics for classifying the books:

   (i) Language.
   (ii) Form.
   (iii) Author.
   (iv) Work.

Under each language by form—poetry, drama, fiction, etc., under each form by authors and finally by individual works. It is most relevant sequence.

CC — Poetry, Drama, Fiction.

DC — Language, Form, Period, Author-sequence.

There should be more than one characteristics which give relevant result.

Example: Books—when we use certain subject where we use space followed by time. The two relevant characteristics have been used in succession:

Geographical area: Relevant characteristics would be by

geographical division, i.e. lake, mountain, author; by environment factors, i.e. climate.

Author by political, territorial distribution.

Author by history, i.e. nation.

3.4.3 Canon of Consistent Succession

Lack of consistency leads to confusion and defeats the purpose of classification.

There should be consistency in same sequence.

Example: Literature—

DC., CC Language, form, author, work whether books are in Hindi, Tamil, English others language.

CC. Law.

Main class: Zoology: 'species of animals'
'organs of animals'
as successive characteristics.

3.5 Canons of Array

An array is defined as "a sequence of coordinate classes of a universe derived from it on the basis of characteristics and arranged among themselves according to their ranks."

World

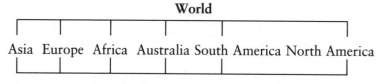

Asia Europe Africa Australia South America North America

Single characteristic (same rank)

They are arranged according to their nearness and are coordinated. Hence, they are known as array of classes.

000	Generalities	500	Pure Science
100	Philosophy	600	Technology
200	Religion	700	Arts
300	Social Science	800	Literature
400	Language	900	Geography and History

2nd order of array

510 Maths

560 Paleontology

520 Astronomy

Life Sciences   570

530 Physics

Botanical Class   580

540 Chemistry

Zoological Sciences   590

550 Earth Science

Further division of facets is next order of array.

3rd array
Medicine

1. Regional organ   5. Genito-urinary system
2. Digestive system   6. Ductless glands
3. Circulatory System   7. Nervous system
4. Respiratory System   8. Other systems.

4th array
Respiratory System

41 Nose   44 Bronhci
42 Larynx   45 Lung.
43 Trachea

Every stage of division is an array based on the same kind of characteristics.

There are four essential requisites to be satisfied in the sequence to be called an Array of classes. These are four canons:

    (a) Canon of exhaustiveness.

    (b) Canon of exclusiveness.

    (c) Canon of helpful sequence.

    (d) Canon of consistent sequence.

3.5.1 Canon of Exhaustiveness

This canon demands that while classifying a universe nothing should be left out. Every entity comprised in the immediate universe should find a place in one of the classes in the array derived from the immediate universe.

Every entity

(i) should find a place in one of the classes;

(ii) a class in the array derived from the immediate universe.

Example:

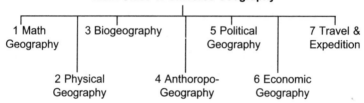

Main Class of Universe Geography

| 1 Math Geography | 3 Biogeography | 5 Political Geography | 7 Travel & Expedition |

| 2 Physical Geography | 4 Anthoropo-Geography | 6 Economic Geography |

All these seven classes are coordinated among themselves, and derived from personality facet of the main class Geography on the basis of single characteristic:

(i) Coordination among the classes.

(ii) Denied from personality facet of main class.

(iii) Based on single characteristics.

All these seven classes and their sub-classes should not be omitted.

Example:

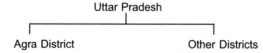

Uttar Pradesh

| Agra District | Other Districts |

Canon of exhaustiveness is satisfied to a great extent by the arrays being kept upon with the help of:

(i) Sector Notation;

(ii) Devices like Subject device, Chronological device, Geographical device and Alphabetical device; and

(iii) An array should accommodate any number of coordinate classes according to the needs.

Precautions: Best method is to leave gaps, so that whenever, or in further a classification sub-class is fully recognised, it is duly accounted for.

3.5.2 Canon of Exclusiveness

It has following special features :

(i) An entity considered to be a sub-division of one class should not be considered as a sub-division of another class.

(ii) No two classes of an array should overlap.

(iii) No two classes have an entity in common.

(iv) If any of the entities are common to two or more classes, the canon of exclusiveness is violated.

Example: Students are grouped on the basis of five characteristics—sex, age, height, weight, mother tongue.

Each of these classes can be further divided into several classes on the basis of some other characteristics. All the sub-classes will have to be derived on the basis of a different single characteristics.

Ramkrishna   Male
                              20 years of age.
                              1mt. 55cms. height.
                              Weight 45kg.
                              Malayalam, mother tongue.

One entity is considered to be a sub-division of several classes of an array.

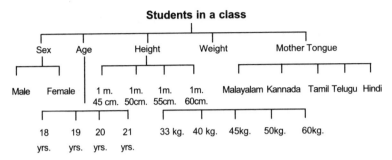

Violation of the canon

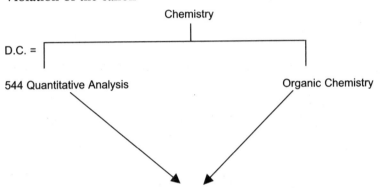

Quantitative analysis of organic substance

Example:

This is cross classification and use of more than one characteristics – characteristics of quantitative analysis and also organic chemistry.

CC

S. Psychology (P)	T. Education (P)	Y. Sociology (P)
1. Child	1. Pre-secondary	1. By age and sex
2. Adolescent	2. Secondary	2. Family
3. Post Adolescent	3. Adult	3. By residence
4. Vocational	4. University	4. By occupation
5. Sex	5. Sex	5. By birth or status
6. Abnormal	6. Abnormal	6. Abnormal
7. Race	7. Backward class	7. Race as a social group
8. Social	8. Other classes	8. By association
9. Animal		9. Others

We may divide literature in two characteristics, i.e. by form and 'by country'.

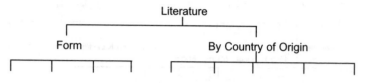

3.5.3 Application of Helpful Sequence in an Array

The canon of helpful sequence demands that classes in an array should be arranged in a helpful manner. If there are four classes in an array, there will be 1x2x3x4=24 possible sequences. How to determine that one particular sequence is most helpful than the remaining 23 sequences. We may organise the subjects of different extensions in a helpful sequence. The principle of decreasing extension will help us.

How to decide the sequence between the coordinate classes, which make an array, in regard to their characteristics and relations, interest and purpose.

Richardson's Principles: Richardson has proposed 9 principles which are presented as under:

1. Logical Principle — From complex to the simplest.
2. Geometrical — Position of items in space.
3. Chronological — Position according to time.
4. Genetic Principle — Per likeness in origin.
5. Historical — Combination of preceding.
6. Evolutionary Principle — From simple to complex.
7. Dynamic — Sequence of power.
8. Alphabetical Principle.
9. Mathematical sequence through the value of notation.

We can analyse them as under:

Principle 1, 6 are opposite to each other.

Principle 2, 3, 8, 9 are simple to determine and useful.

Principle 4, 5, 7 are difficult to determine.

3.5.4 Hospitality in Array in Notation

The field of knowledge has grown enormously. It is ever growing. All items of knowledge are accommodated in arrays of different orders.

Characteristics: The array in notation should be hospitable. It should be able to accommodate any number of coordinate classes.

DC used Arabic numbers for notation. It is most useful in case of arrays of isolates and its order.

CC also used it, but it is limited to 1 to 9. But we find that coordinate classes in many arrays are much more than nine in number. This has raised the crisis in notation.

(a) **Canon of Interpolation in Array:** An array of class numbers or of isolate numbers should admit of the interpolation of any member of new coordinate numbers at any point in the array.

> **Gap Device:** Gaps are left to accommodate new classes.

Lz3	Pharmacology	Lz4
Lz5	Pharmacopoeia	Lz6
Lz8	Pharmacy	Lz7

(b) **Sector Device and Group Notation:** Digit 9 is not used in the concept of decimal fraction notation.

1, 2, 3, 4, 5, 6, 7, 8, 91, 92, 93, 94, 95, 96, 97, 98, 991, 992, 993, 994, 995, 996, 997, 998, 9991, 9992, and so on.

1st sector	2nd sector	3rd sector	4th sector	5th sector	6th sector
1	91	991	9991	99991	999991
2	92	992	9992	99992	999992
3	93	993	9993	99993	999993
4	94	994	9994	99994	999994
5	95	995	9995	99995	999995
6	96	996	9996	99996	999996
7	97	997	9997	99997	999997
8	98	998	9998	99998	999998

Group 1 Utility array	Group 2 Plant part array	Group 3 Species of plant array
1 Decoration	1 Sap	1 ⎫ Used for
2 Feed	2 Bulb	2 ⎪ individualising
3 Food	3 Root	3 ⎪ particular species
4 Stimulant	4 Stem	4 ⎬ of a plant
5 Oil	5 Leaf	5 ⎪
6 Drug	6 Flower	6 ⎪
7 Fabric	7 Fruit	7 ⎪
8 Dye, Tan	8 Seed	8 ⎭
91 Adhesive	97 Whole plant	
92 Manure		
93 Vegetable		
94 Sugar producing		

There are other devices which are common in CC.

(c) **Chronological Device:** 0111, 1228/0111, 3L28.

(d) **Alphabetical Device.**

(e) **Common Isolate Device:** Aa Bb Ca Da (Bibliographics).

(f) **Zone Analysis:** It provides for great hospitality in any order of arrays. It may be the order of main classes; such isolates or any further lower order.

The concept is dependent on the use of mixed notation.

   (i) ECI—Enumerative Common Isolate—

      A, b, c, d, e, f, g .... (lower case alphabets).

  (ii) ESI—Enumerative Special Isolate

      Arabic numbers. 1, 2, 3, 4, 5, 6, 7, 8 in decimal numbers.

 (iii) DSI—Devised Special Isolates

      Capital alphabets A, B, C, D, E, F, G, H .... X, Y, Z.

      Numbers in brackets. ( ) (.)

(g) **Subject Device:** This represents a subject.

DC—'Device like' 000-999

CC-1. Psychology of University teachers S4 (T4)

    2. Hindu Ethics   R4 (Q2)

    3. Industrial Microbiology.

F: (G91)

(h) Geographical Device—This represents area.

Indian Painting	NQ 44
Indian Music	N4 44
Indian History	V 44
Indian Law	Z 44.

Principles for Chain

The term chain in the classification of knowledge stands for a sequence of classes, not coordinate among themselves, where the second class in the chain is derived from the first class, the third class is derived from the second and fourth class is derived from the third class in the chain, and so on.

Chain:		Social Science
↓	B	Maths
↓	B2	Algebra
↓	B28	Statistics
↓	B281	Probability
↓	B2813	Normal Equation.

The schedule of the chain is worked out in a disciplined manner.

There are two canons.

4.1 Canon of Decreasing Extension

While moving down a chain from its first link to its last, the extension of the classes or of the ranked isolates, as the case may be, should decrease and the intention should increase at each step.

The extension of a class is measured:

(a) By the number of entities.

(b) Or the range comprised in the class.

(c) Or in the ranked isolate.

While its intention is measured: number of characteristics used in deriving the class forms the original universe.

In other words: (a) Extension is quantitative measure.

(b) Intention is qualitative measure of a class.

It is the principle that:

Broader the class, fewer are the attributes.

Greater the extension, the smaller will be the intention.

The concept of decreasing extension has been equated with the

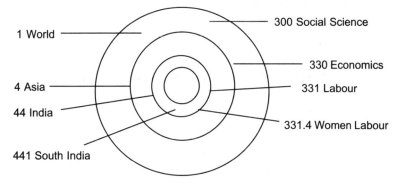

principle of general before special. Major comes before minor.

4.2 Canon of Modulation

The chain of classes or of ranked isolates should comprise one class or one ranked isolate, as the case may be, of each and every order that lies between the orders of the first link and the last link of the chain.

No link in between a chain of classes be left out. Father should come in between grandfather and grandson.

Chain 1		Chain 2	
1	World	1	World
4	Asia	4	Asia
44	India	44	India
		441	South India
4412	Kerala	4412	Kerala
(Best Modulated sequence)		(Not Modulated sequence)	

Modular should depend on:

1. Relevant characteristics allowed in a train of characteristics.

2. Sequence of application of those characteristics.

Hospitality in Chain in Notation: A subject specialisation generally covers minor areas. In a chain, one finds one facet of the class divisible by one or more other facets of the same class. It needs them in notation to individualise the document.

4.3 Canon of Extrapolation

Various devices have been invented by the profession:

(a) **Decimal Fraction Device:** Every number in notation is considered as a pure decimal fraction. Just as a class is divisible into various subclasses, in the same manner the translated ordinal number should also be subdivisible. This can conveniently be done with the help of Decimal Fraction notation.

Science 5

500	510	520	530	540	550	560	570	580	590
Pure Science	Maths	Astronomy	Physics	Chemistry	Earth Sc.	Paleontology	Anthropology	Botany	Zoology

Example: A series of 1, 2, 3 --------8, 9 can be extended to 1, 2, 21, 22, 23—3-8, 9, 91, 92--------- and so on. Similarly, letters are also used in fraction. Any class can be divided indefinitely.

(b) Gap Device: In the context of extrapolation in chain use of the numbers left unused after a particular number in an array, as if they are subdivisions of that number, it is called 'Gap Device'. The device violates the canon of hierarchical. It satisfies the canon of extrapolation in chain only to a very limited extent.

CC and DC both treat each number consisting of Arabic numerals as a pure decimal fraction:

— But decimal point is not used.

— Decimal point is considered to be understood before every number.

— A new class is treated in a chain by subdividing the class forming its last link on the basis of a new additional characteristics.

— Any such class forming out of subdividing the classified on a characteristic, can be added to a chain.

Decimal fraction device gives:

(a) A distinct class number.

(b) A helpful class number to each new subordinate class in a chain, because :

   (i) it provides for addition of digits at the end of the chain;

   (ii) it does not disturb the ordinal value of any existing class number. Hence, decimal fraction device was brought into popular use by DC and later by CC.

DC: 300 Social Science

            330 Economics

            331 Labour Economics

            331.137 Unemployment

            331.1378 Unemployment in specific occupation

            331.13782 Unemployment of engineers.

Hospitality in chain is secured in manifold infinity of links because of the facet analysis employed in it.

Separate characteristics:

(a) Unemployment in specific occupations.

(b) Unemployment among engineers.

(c) Unemployment among engineers in India.

In CC decimal fraction device secures hospitality in chain in several directions:

(a) Unemployment in industries × 8(A): 95851

(b) Unemployment in industry in India × 8(A): 95851.44

Unemployment in Engg. industries in India x 8(D): 95851.44
CC provides extensive class numbers for all titles.

Canon of Interpolation: A chain of class numbers or of isolate numbers should admit of the interpolation of any number of links between two consecutive links in the chain.

Empty Digit: Empty digit normally in use are z, 9 and Z. Each of them is empty in the sense that:

(a) It does not represent any specific focal idea: (Specific BC).

(b) It has only ordinal value.

(c) Its ordinal value is its only semantic content.

5

Canon of Helpful Sequence

5.1 Concept of Helpful Sequence

The main purpose of classification is helpful sequence :

— Like things are put together while unlike things are put separately.
— The need in classification of knowledge is to maintain a helpful sequence between the various divisions of knowledge.
— Structure of knowledge is so complicated that it is very difficult to maintain helpful sequence.
— There are no foolproof standards or principles through which helpful sequence could be maintained.
— Thoughts in documents are generally multiple classes as against one single class.
— It needs their relations. (Mutual) Nations are recognised or individualised.

Bliss: He suggested two principles of utmost importance:

1. Subordination of special (or specific) to relevant general(or generic) classes; and
2. Collocation (placing) of closely related classes, subordinate and coordinate.

Sayers: He suggested two terms:

1. Extension.
2. Intention.

He further elaborates:

(a) Right subordination of subjects.

(b) Correct coordination of subject.

(c) Right placing (collocated) of each class.

Ranganathan analysed the problem and put a chapter in elements of classification (1944) on Helpful Sequence.

Division of knowledge in coordinate groups of classes are array and (in subordination) chain. And by principle of greater extension before the lesser extension for helpful sequence.

Need for helpful sequence:

1. Like things to put together.
2. Unlike things to put aside.
3. To make the classification more effective.
4. To put various divisions of knowledge in helpful sequence.
5. Structure of knowledge is complicated, hence necessary to make it easy by helpful sequence.
6. There is no foolproof standard to maintain helpful sequence.
7. Thoughts of documents are multiple and complicated, hence need of helpful sequence.
8. To maintain mutual relations between classes.

Definitions: Helpful sequence may be maintained by two principles:

(a) Subordination of special (specific) to relevant general (generic) classes.

(b) Collocation of closely related classes, subordinate (placing) and coordinate.

Ranganathan has given the following principles influencing helpful sequence:

1. Principle of decreasing extension.
2. Principle of increasing concreteness.
3. Principle of later in evolution.
4. Principle of later in time.
5. Principle of spatial contiguity.
6. Principle of canonical sequence.

7. Principle of consistent sequence.
8. Principle of increasing complexity.
9. Principle of alphabetical sequence.

In addition to principles, a number of situations arise where these principles are found ineffective.

Group 1	Group 2	Group 3
1. University education	3. Teaching technique in education	5. Teaching technique in university.
2. Secondary school	4. Curriculum	6. Curriculum in education university.
		7. Curriculum in Secondary Schools.
		8. Teaching technique in Secondary Schools.

5.2 Principle of Decreasing Extension

Extension of a class is measured by the number of entities, while its intention is measured by the number of characteristics used in deriving the class from the original universe. Extension is a quantitative measure of a class.

Intention is a qualitative measure of a class.

Sayers says: Broader the class, fewer are the attributes.

Greater the extension, the smaller will be intention.

Greater the extension, the smaller will be intention.

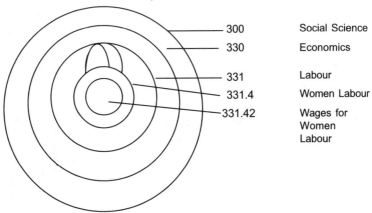

300	Social Science
330	Economics
331	Labour
331.4	Women Labour
331.42	Wages for Women Labour

5.3 Principle of Increasing Quantity/Concreteness

If the subject in an array of subjects or the isolates in an array of isolates admit of quantitative distinction. They may be arranged according to their increasing quantity, if it is helpful.

5.4 Principle of Later-in-Time.

5.5 Principle of Later-in-Evolution

If the subjects in an array of subjects or the isolates in an array of isolates belong to different stages of evolution, they should be arranged parallel to the evolutionary sequence.

Preference is usually given to the former principles between principal dates in evolution and earlier-in-evolution.

Classifying the universe on the basis of the "Natural Group" as characteristics, i.e. in evolutionary sequence.

Natural Group of Evolution

	Zoology	CC	DC		
Zoology	↓	K	590	Amphibia	K93
Protozoa	↓	K2	593	Reptilia	K94
Porifera	↓	K3	593.4	Aves	K96
Coelenterata	↓	K4	593.5	Mammalia	K97
Echinodermata	↓	K5	593.9		
Vermes	↓	K6	595.1		
Mollusca	↓	K7	594		
Anthropoda	↓	K8	595.2		
Prochordata	↓	K91	596		
Pisces (Fishes)	↓	K92	597		

Example:

Pol. Sc.

Anarchy

Democracy

5.6 Principle of Spatial Contiguity

If subjects in an array of subjects or the isolates in an array of isolates occur contiguously in space—roughly along undirectional linear or a radial line or a circle—they should be arranged in a parallel spatial sequence except when any of the following is already applied :

   (a) Principle of bottom upward.

   (b) Principle of top downward.

   (c) Principle of left to right.

   (d) Principle of right to left.

   (e) Principle of clockwise direction.

   (f) Principle of counter-clockwise direction.

   (g) Principle of periphery to centre.

   (h) Principle of centre to periphery.

   (i) Principle of away from position.

   (j) Principle of increasing quantity.

   (k) Principle of decreasing quantity.

   (l) Principle of increasing complexity.

  (m) Principle of canonical sequence.

   (n) Principle of literary warrant.

   (o) Principle of alphabetical sequence.

5.7 Principle of Canonical Sequence

If the subjects in an array of subjects or the isolates in an array of isolates are traditionally referred to in a specific adequance, although no underlying principle is discoverable, it will be convenient to conform to this traditional sequence.

In CC the traditional divisions of a universe are known as canonical classes (Traditional sequence).

The following arrays are in canonical sequence:

   1. The divisions of main class — Mathematics: Arithmetic, Algebra, Analysis, Trigonometry, Geometry, Mechanics, Polarities and Astronomy.

5.8 Principle of Consistent Sequence

Whenever similar classes occur explicitly (clear and easy to understand) or implicitly in different arrays, they must be arranged in the same sequences in all these arrays. Conformity to the canon of constant sequence will save time and energy. It will minimize the load or the memory—both for the classifier and for the use of the library. This canon is responsible for certain practices and devices in some of the schemes of classification.

There are two ways of securing constant sequence in the scheme:

(a) By using one and the same schedule to form an array in whatever subject they occur.

(b) Maintenance of parallel sequence with the help of principle of helpful sequence.

5.9 Principle of Increasing Complexity

If the subjects in an array of subjects or the isolates in an array of isolates show different degrees of complexity, they should be arranged parallel to the sequence of increasing complexity except when any other overwhelming consideration rules it out.

Fine Art

Town planning

(on the basis of population-cluster as characteristics)

|

(In sequence)

Village planning

Town planning

City planning

Metropolis planning

5.10 Principle of Alphabetical Sequence

When no other sequence of the subjects in an array of subjects or the isolates in an array of isolates is more helpful, they may be arranged alphabetically by their names current in international usage.

William Shakespeare:

0111,2 J64, H   Hamlet

0111,2 J64, J   Julius Ceaser

0111,2 J64,	K	King Lear
0111,2 J64,	M	Macbeth
324.2454	B	Bhartiya Janata Party
324.2454	C	Communist Party of India

Palmer and Wells have defined helpful sequence in the following manner:

> "Helpful order (sequence) can be defined as that which displays subjects in such a way that a person approaching a group of subjects at any point is led by the order (sequence) itself to the specific subject he needs."

They feel that such a sequence can be established with the principle of decreasing extension. It is suggested that the following sequence be maintained:

(a) The general treated generally.
(b) The general treated specially.
(c) The special treated generally.
(d) The special treated specially.

5.11 APUPA Pattern

There are three types of records:

UMBRAL Record: A totally or intimately relevant record is known as Umbral Record.

PENUMBRAL Record: A partially irrelevant (but in some manner related Umbral) record is known as Penumbral record.

ALIEN Record: A totally irrelevant (in no manner related to the Umbral) is known as Alien record.

Arrangement in helpful sequence:

| Alien (Not relevant) | Penumbral (Less relevant record) | Umbral (most relevant record) | Penumbral (less relevant record) | Alien (Not relevant) |

The implications of helpful sequence in a scheme of knowledge classification are in five directions:

(a) Sequence between the traditional main classes.
(b) Sequence between the various facets of a main class.

(c) Sequence between the isolates of a facet which falls in an array.

(d) Sequence between the isolates of a facet which fall in a chain.

(e) Sequence between the common and special isolates.

General Concepts of APUPA pattern helps:

(a) In the case of principle of increasing concreteness.

(b) In the case of the isolates arrangement with the help of the principle of evolution, time, spatial contiguity, canonical sequence and increasing complexity.

(c) In case of the principle of decreasing extension for validity of arrangement.

(d) In case of common isolates in sorting out for those which demand:

    (i) Placement before (anteriorising).

    (ii) Placement after (posteriorising) the special isolates with the help of the above principles, it is possible for a scheme of classification to provide helpful sequence in the organisation of documents. The principles discussed above are logical and can satisfy all approaches.

5.11.1 Filiatory Arrangement

Filiatory arrangement is the placement of all the entities of a universe in a definite sequence in one line according to the degree of their mutual affinities. This definite sequence is achieved after complete sorting out (assortment) of the divisions of classes under consideration. The feature of this arrangement is ranking according to the degree of relation, i.e.:

1. The subdivision of a class having first rank relation with a subject will come first.

2. The second place will go to the subjects of second rank relation and their divisions.

3. Then will come the third related subject with its divisions and so on.

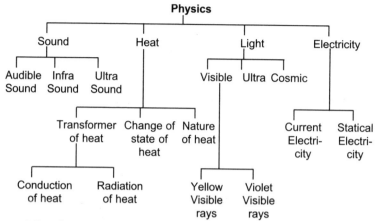

The classes arranged are in helpful sequence.

5.11.2 Canon of Consistent Sequence

When similar classes or ranked isolates occur in different arrays, their sequence should be parallel in such arrays, whenever assistance on such parallelism does not run counter to other more important requirements.

There are two ways of securing consistent sequence:

(a) Schedule of common Isolates of Devices.

(b) Principle of helpful sequence.

DC   (a) 'Add to' device.

DC/CC   (b) Standard subdivisions.

          (c) Areas.

          (d) Subdivisions of individual literatures.

          (e) Subdivisions of individual languages.

          (f) Racial.

          (g) Language.

          (h) Persons.

6

Five Fundamental Categories

Main class: Any class enumerated in the first order array of a scheme of classification of the universe of knowledge. Main classes are the major divisions of the universe of knowledge.

Categories: Once the knowledge is organised into a number of main classes and further in facets, categories are made.

Steps:

(a) Main class

(b) Dividing the main class in different sub-classes, facets falls within it.

(c) Each facet in its fundamental categories. (Every facet is an isolate idea. It is sorted out and arranged in helpful sequence).

(d) Further division is processed and the isolates to each fundamental categories are enumerated.

(e) Isolates are divided up to 5th or 6th step in the process of division.

Five fundamental categories

Main class or canonical class

1. Personality
2. Matter
3. Energy
4. Space
5. Time.

Important concepts

1. Main class
2. Facet under a subject
3. Isolates in facets and their subdivision
4. Classes in array
5. Classes in a chain.

Main class → Division on the basis → Facet
                of chain of characteristics

Facet L: The term facet is used at a particular stage in the process of the division of the universe of knowledge.

There is no facet up to main class.

Concept of facet appears while dividing the main class. Main class has :

(a) Smaller units of ideas/entities within it.

(b) Groups all divisions/entities of one characteristics.

(c) Individualisation of entities under different facets of a subject.

Entities of Psychology: The following are the entities of psychology:

> **Psychology**
> Sensation
> Sex
> Adolescence
> Personality
> Abnormal
> Nervous system
> Emotion
> Child.

The sequence may be one.

If there are nine units, the possible number of sequences will be $1 \times 2 \times 3 \times 4 \times 5 \times 6 \times 7 \times 8 \times 9 = 3,62,880$.

1	12	121	122
11	121	1211	1221
111	122	12111	12211
1111	123	121111	122111
11111	124	1211111	1221111
111111	125	12111111	12211111
1111111	126	121111111	122111111
11111111	127	1211111111	1221111111

Individualisation of facets:

Psychology

Facet I	**Facet II**
Sex	Sensation
Adolescence	Cognition
Abnormal	Personality
Child	Nervous system
	Emotion

Main class is:

   (a) First grouped under each possible category.

   (b) Then individualised on the basis of :

      (i) certain train of characteristics;

      (ii) a certain number of trains of characteristics will yield a equal number of facets of a class.

Facet is a totality of the isolates formed on the basis of a single train of characteristics in a facet.

Facets are derived out of main class by facet analysis.

6.1 Facet Analysis

Facet analysis is a tool for the organisation of ideas. Division of knowledge must proceed from the general to the particular by assembling under each class, terms of less extension that comprise the class and grouping them into categories or facets.

Facet analysis means enumeration of the possible trains of characteristics by which a main class can be divided. Facet analysis is an application of different characteristics. Within a facet a single division or an individual sub-class is called a focus.

Example: Hindi literature is a focus in the language facet.

DC— English Poetry is a focus in the literary form facet of the English literature.

In case the sub-class consists of more than one focus, it is called compound subject.

Example: Literature—Hindi poetry—combine two foci-one (compound subject) from language and then from literary form.

There are five fundamental categories:

P—Personality

M—Matter

E—Energy

S—Space

T—Time.

6.1.1 Personality

It is of first importance in many of the subjects of any class.

The entity which forms the focus of study in all the subjects going with a main subject may be called the 'core component'.

Palmer: The term 'personality' is used for the wholeness of any subject.

Mill: The term personality is used to describe those facets of any subject which are generally unique to that subject and which give it its essential character or personality.

In short, the personality of a subject will be a vital area which forms the body of the subject or makes its basic structure.

Without personality there can be no organ, constituent, attribute, action, etc.

Any main class where categories are applicable may have the personality facet.

Example: Agriculture   —   Crops
                Medicine   —   Human body
                Chemistry   —   Substance
                Botany   —   Plants
                Zoology   —   Animals
                Literature   —   Language name

Level: There are number of levels into which whole personality is spread. These are known as levels of personality.

P1, P2, P3, P4

Levels are arranged with the help of the principle of helpful sequence:

Main class	DC	Personality Facet	CC
Psychology	150	Abnormal Psychology	S6
Economics	330	Public Finance	*7
Chemistry	540	Inorganic Chemistry	E1

Level of Personality

Main class	P1	P2	P3	P4
Literature	Language	Form	Author	His work

Example: Libraries may be divided into:

(a) Ownership (Public, Private, etc.).

(b) Educational status (School, University, etc.).

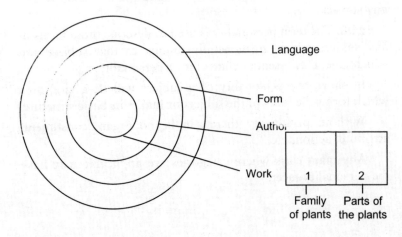

    (c) Physical status of the user (Hospital, Patient, Blinds).

    (d) Subject covered (Chemistry, Medicines, etc.).

6.1.2 Matter

Mill: Matter is a category of facets which reflects substances, materials, etc. It is absent from theoretical disciplines like Law, Economics, Literature.

Vickrey: Matter comprises constituent materials of all kinds.

Palmer and Wells: Classifying books on manufacture of paper, some divisions are based on the raw material, substance, commodity.

Example: Building material

                    Building + Material

                             (matter)

6.1.3 Energy

Energy covers:

    (a) Problems

    (b) Actions

    (c) Methods

    (d) Functioning.

These are the aspects of main class.

Energy is a facet of category which characterise the exercise of energy, i.e. activities, operations, processes, problems, etc.

Many main classes have certain units which deal with the problems in the subject. These problems are generally applicable to all the organs of the class.

Example:

Agriculture — Sowing, Harvesting   ⎤ deals with

Medicine — Physiology, Pathology   ⎦ functioning

Energy covers generally the important problems of the subjects and commands a great influence on the subject from two directions.

Further classification of energy deals with common energy isolates—

(a) Intellectual activities
(b) Industrial activities   These are common
(c) Institutional activities   to all

Main Class	Energy Facet	DC	CC
Botany	Plant Physiology	581.1	1:3
Botany	Plant Pathology	581.2	1:4
Botany	Plant Morphology	581.4	1:2
Education	Curriculum	375	T:Z
History	Foreign Relations	327	V:19

The energy may manifest itself in one and the same subject more than once.

This manifestation is turned (around) as:

(a) Second round energy (2E).

(b) Third round energy (3E).

The second and third round energy is based on "wall picture principle", which means a facet depending on another facet for its very existence should come after that other facet. The sequence will be:

[E] [2E]   [3E]

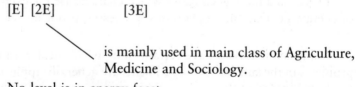

is mainly used in main class of Agriculture, Medicine and Sociology.

No level is in energy facet.

6.1.4 Space

It is one of the important facets of main class. Most of the subjects, if not all, get manifested in relation with continents, countries and their subdivisions.

In other words, space is the manifestation of the surface of the earth, the space inside it, and the space outside it. This includes continents and cities (geographical areas).

6.1.5 Time

Time is a simple concept/facet. It indicates that the entities under different subjects must go on changing in the structure, meaning, history, development, etc. Subjects get expanded differently with the progress of time.

Time occurs under every main class, so all possible divisions of time including century, decade, year, month, day, hours, etc.

CC. Chronological Table (time facet)

DC. Used under class History, Literature

Example: International ors in 1925 (Time facet)

Sequence between different levels:

Personality facet   ,

Matter facet   ;

Energy facet   :

Space facet   .

Time facet   '

Method of Residue: (Neti – Neti principle)

(Not-This-Not-This principle)

— A kernel idea is correlated with each of the four fundamental categories: [T] [S] [E] [M] in succession.

If the kernel idea is not manifested in any of these four fundamental categories, it will be manifested in fundamental category [P].

Isolates

Isolate: We can divide isolates in two categories:

1. Common Isolates.
2. Special Isolates.

Isolate is a generic term to denote isolate idea, isolate term or isolate number.

Each division in a facet is said to be an isolate focus or simply an isolate. It is equally used in all the three planes.

7.1 Common Isolates

A blind tradition has persisted through general decades in regard to the schedule of common isolate or such divisions or form division. These are enumerated in main class.

Common subdivisions are applied to all main classes. As is clear from the names, they are common to all.

For the first time (c1) common isolates (CI) were used by DC as formed division by Dewey in 1876 in his decimal classification.

> DC — Form Division
>
> CC — Common Isolates

Some say that form divisions are not common isolates as they were not used with all main classes until and unless directed.

Cutter: For the first time Cutter (1891) in his Expensive Classification had a local list of common isolates.

Brown provided a schedule of 'categorical table'.

CC did not used any list of (CI) in his first edition in 1933.

Common isolates are those minor units in the structure of knowledge which are represented by the same term and by the same number wherever they occur in a scheme of classification.

Ranganathan defines it as "Common isolate: Isolate idea represented by the same isolate term and same isolate number in more or less every class having it."

Common isolate is an old feature of classification.

Dewey recognised it as form division.

Bliss turned them as anterior and ancillary.

Brown maintained the principles of common isolates, but he also listed those isolates which were common only to a few and not to all.

Bliss says, "these are systematic (common) not only in the ordinary sense but in that they are applicable more or less extensively throughout the system. Some may be applicable, wholly or partly, under any class, others only under certain classes or sections".

Sayers says, "Certain of these methods of treatment are common to every subject and a series of form divisions to individualise them has been attached to most library classification.

Cutter	—	Local list
Brown	—	Categorical division
DC	—	Form division
CC	—	Common isolates (Approach material)
UDC	—	Various forms.

7.2 Types of Common Isolates (CI)

Every scheme used common isolates with their own interpretations and formulated common isolates (CI) in different categories.

7.2.1 UDC

		Notations
1.	Common Auxiliaries of language	=
2.	Common Auxiliaries of form	(0.....)
3.	Common Auxiliaries of place	(1) to (9)
4.	Common Auxiliaries of race & nationality	(=....)
5.	Common Auxiliaries of time	"
6.	Alphabetical & Numerical subdivision	
7.	Common Auxiliaries of point of view	.00
8.	Special subdivisions	-0/-9,.0 and ' .....

7.2.2 CC

1. Anteriorising Common Isolates (Applicable Before Space Facet) (ACIBSF)
2. Anteriorising Common Isolates (Applicable After Space Facet) (ACIASF)
3. Anteriorising Common Isolate (Applicable After the Time Facet) (ACIAATI)
4. Posteriorising Common Isolate (Energy Common Isolates) (PCIECI)
5. Posteriorisiong Common Isolate (Personality Common Isolate) (PCIPCI)
6. Miscellaneous Common Isolates
   (a) Space Isolates (SI)
   (b) Time Isolates (TI)
   (c) Physiological Common Isolates (PhCI).

DC: Form divisions

13th ed.	One zero
17th	.0
	.00
	.000

CC: Common isolates are used according to their characteristics.

1. If ACI before space – No symbol.
   It is attached with host class always.
2. If ACI after space – No symbol.
   Attached with (SI) space isolates.
3. If ACI after time 1 – No symbol.
   It is attached with time facet.
4. If PCI — Energy (CI) = : Colon.
5. If PCI — Personality (CI) = , Comma

Base:

DC — Pure base

UDC — Sign, Symbols (IAN), Pockets and Roman Capital

CC — Roman Small and (IAN)

Types of CI

1. Physical form of Document — Collection No.
2. Language, form of exposition, mutual relation etc. of documents — Book No.
3. Document which it helped to arrange interior to ordinary — Interior Common Isolates.
4. Thought contents of document — Posteriorising Common Isolates.

7.2.2.1 Anteriorising Common Isolates (ACI)

ACI: ACI means the material having interior position in a main class. Ranganathan calls it "approach material", like reference books, textbooks, encyclopaedias, bibliography, case study, etc.

CC: CC secures anteriorising position to approach material by representing an anteriorisiong isolate in its class number by 9. Roman small 'a' has interiorising value — e.g. Bibliography of Astronomy — B9 a.

They are directly attached without any connecting symbol as the attachment of connection necessarily leads to the posterior value. Moreover, they possess their own facet formula.

Example: Application before space facet:

Bibliography on Mathematics   Ba

Dictionary of Mechanical Engg.   D6k

[P] Facet is brought by (GD) and [P2] facet by (CD)

Herald of Library Science   2m44, N62

Here India is [P] and 1962 year of origin of periodical is [P2].

Applicable only after space facet:

Annual report of education in India (1970).

T. 44r 'N70

Applicable only after time facet:

Report of Advisory Committee for libraries.

2.44 'N59t

History of Bibliography of Civil Engineering in India brought up to 1970's.

DIav 44 'N7

7.2.2.2 Posteriorising Common Isolates

Five types: Time, Space, Energy, Matter, Personality

Literary Criticism   0:g

Criticism of Shakespeare   0111,2J64:g

— A personality PCI should generally be added after space facet. A list of personality PCIs is given in CC at page No. 2.6. The personality PCI is having its own facet formula, i.e. C1, [P1], [P2]

Indian librarianship $\longrightarrow$ 2.44,b

Generally all time and space isolates come under(PCI). They are applied or used generally after host class itself. The insertion connecting digit of (PCI) of the host class or at the position of space and time indicates (PCI).

BC: In the scheme time isolate is not made Common

Isolate while (SI) has been treated as (CI). For each subject, a time schedule is constructed. It is in one digit.

CC: It is in three digit minimum.

UDC: It has also applied (PC1) in three digits.

1. In CC (ACI) have been used as personality common isolate or we may call them the (I) isolate to be attached with all facets except time and space isolates, while in UDC these are attachable in the every facet or phase.

2. CC has enumerated (ACI) on the concept of the main classes and enriches them with mnemonic qualities:

a   Bibliography

k   Encyclopaedia

v   History.

They are also to be used with their formulas already announced in the schedule, while in CC they have divided (AC1) in main parts by:

(1) Arrangement

(2) Alphabetically

(3) Lectures and addresses

(4) Periodical publications

(5) Publication of bodies

(6) Study books

(7) Collected and selected books

(8) Historical sources.

Though the UDC schedule is enumerative and not of practical approach as there are several points mentioned for more than once in a schedule, e.g. (022) Medium textbooks, (075) School textbooks.

There is little or avoidable difference between two isolates. It makes no difference or put difficulty if textbook in general is used.

CC has enumerated in concise form. It has avoided being homonymous with the help that (ACI) or all (CI) are based on five fundamental concepts. Every isolate is unique at its place and is not repeated. No doubt the facet formula of every particular (CI) may create some confusion to a layman but it guides the classifier to a main target.

3. UDC has not enumerated all the language being used throughout the world. It has avoided Asian language to some extent, which makes this scheme more unpopular, while CC has enumerated all languages being used even in the small country in every corner of the world.

4. One of the interior values of main class (MC), UDC does not recognise them as such in practice. It uses (CI) like (SD) in CC which these do not hold the position of the subject. 332.53(054)

It will be more concrete if these are attached to the host class without pockets.

CC uses them properly and allots them their own position.

5. In CC any Common Isolate has been allotted in the mixed notation—Roman small and Arabic numerals as secondary element. In some place Roman Capital has also been used.

a   Bibliography

y1   Programme of instruction

D   1 to 999 AD

99M   Solresal (Artificial language).

While in UDC (IAN) have taken use for citing Common Isolate (CI) with pocket. Pocket has no cementic value. It is just to make the isolate (I) most attractive.

6. Common Isolate (CI) in CC are co-extensive pinpointed and co-existensive, while UDC violates it by enumerating all isolates without any plan.

CI Concept is an important concept. A classification scheme cannot be flexible until and unless it uses (CI) of various natures with various positions or their status. Simply enumeration will also not be helpful.

7.2.2.3 Space Isolates

Total entries of space isolates are 6000 out of which

94.2%	—	Continents & their subdivisions
1.8%	—	Other portions of the world
4.2%	—	Near world formation
0.6%	—	Sub-formation
0.7%	—	Expire formation
0.2%	—	Land sea formation
0.1%	—	Climate zone formation.

This survey makes the following sequence based on prominence:

CC		UDC
Empire	Continent and its subdivisions	Land (Area)
Zone (Area)	Near world formation	Orientation
Orientation	Other position of the world	Political area
Near for rigu -	Other position of the world	Destination
Formation.....		
Continents.....	Empire formation	Physiological
Land sea formation.	Sub-formation	Ocean
Ocean land	Land sea formation	Ancient world
Physiological	Climate zone formation	Modern world
Formation.....		Continent

Continents may be further subdivided as under:

CC		UDC
Area	Continent	Europe
United Kingdom	Country	United Kingdom
Russia	States	Germany
Africa	Districts	Hungary
North America	Sovereign countries	Italy
Canada		Spain
Australia	Constituent states	Portugal
		Russia
		Sweden
		Switzerland
		Asia
		Africa
		North America
		South America
		Australia

Notation of space

CC		UDC
1	World	1
5	Europe	4
4	Asia	5
6	Africa	6
7	America	7
8	Australia	94

In view of the above tables it is clear that:

1. Both schemes have not followed the principle of special contiguity fully, both have violated the canon of currency.

2. CC has accepted Australia as continent while UDC has not accepted it as continent. UDC has accepted it as Inland.

3. CC starts with Asia. It has given more importance to Asia than Europe because of its longest area in the world, while UDC has started with Europe being its own continent.

Principles of space isolate:

1. Principle of spatial contiguity
2. Principle of clockwise direction
3. Principle of anti-clockwise direction
4. Principle of bottom-upper (South to North)
5. Principle of upward to downward (North to South)
6. Principle of right to left (East to West)
7. Principles of left to right (West to East)

1. Principle of spatial contiguity: CC has followed this principle up to some extent while UDC has not followed it wholly.

Both CC and UDC have not followed the proper sequence.

2. Principle of clockwise direction: Both violated the canon of clockwise direction as they have disrupted the direction in the

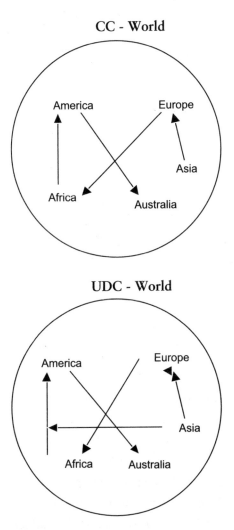

CC - World

UDC - World

way. The direction should be in the way—Asia, Europe, America, Africa and Australia or Europe, America, Africa, Australia & Asia.

3. **Principle of anti-clockwise direction**: If they follow anti-clockwise, the direction would have been the following:

Asia, Australia, Africa, America, Europe, Asia, Australia, Africa and America.

4. Principle of bottom-upper: Both followed the principle of south to north.

CC   -   Asia to Europe

Both -   Africa to America

5. Principle of North to South:

CC   -   It has not followed the principle

UDC -   Europe to Asia

6. Principle of East to West:

CC   -   Europe to Africa

UDC -   Asia to Africa

7. Principle of West to East:

CC   -   America to Australia

UDC -   America to Australia.

Country:

Sequence —	UDC	CC
	Eastern	Southern
	Central	United
	Northern	Central
	Western	

World Formation:

CC		UDC
1	World	1
1N	League of Nations	1-6 LE
1N4	United Nations Area	1-6 UN
1N48	Common Wealth Area	1-6 CO

In CC world formation is divided chronologically from the date of establishment, while in UDC alphabetical device has been used

Empire Formation:

CC		UDC
1-0	Empire	41-44 British empire
1-52	Roman Empire	45-44 Roman empire
1-56	British Empire	

CC has divided Roman empire as its subdivision or subordinate of the world, while UDC has put all empires under the name of the country. In this case CC has used the concise way by putting all empires at one place. In UDC all books on empire will be scattered.

Subject formation:

CC	1 (P111)	English speaking countries
	1 (Q 7)	Muslim countries
UDC	1 – 20	English speaking countries
	1 – 914	Muslim countries & other countries

CC has used the subject device, under the subject it will get all books arranged at one place.

UDC has also followed the same principle.

Oceanic formation:

CC	95	Indian Ocean
	96	Atlantic Ocean
	97	Pacific Ocean
UDC	261/264	Atlantic Ocean
	267	Indian Ocean
	265/266	Pacific Ocean

Both schemes have separate provision for ocean formation.

Physiological formation:

CC has used a separate schedule for physiological formation. It has been given the place of second level space (S2). All isolates under this formation are used small Romans with (IAN) as second digit :

Sector — (a-y)	1st Remove	— small Roman	'a'
Sector (91-98)	2nd Remove	— (IAN)	'e6' Island p1 River

UDC—   Mountains (23)

Both have provided separate schedule.

Physical features:

a	Geosphere			g7	Mountain
e5	Delta			j	Hydrosphere
e6	Island			p1	River
f	Forest			p6	Lake
g1	Valley			r	Ocean
c3	Plain			m2	Bay
c4	Desert			n 3	Gulf
m	Coastal area			p2	Stream

Rivers of South India	-	U2.21.p1
Conquest to Kanchanjanga	-	U8.4g7k
Mountaineering	-	U8.g7
Cultivation in Himalayas	-	J.4.g7H
Rainfall in Delhi in 1972	-	U2885.4481 'N72
Library legislation in USA	-	22(Z).73

Favoured country:

Classification of books in the libraries of India	-	2; 43: 61.2
Classification of books in the libraries of China	-	2; 43:51.41
History of Roman Empire		V 1-51

Population cluster:

9A Hamlets		9E	Super Town
9B Villages		9F	Cities
9D Towns		9J	Super Cities
		9M	Extra-Super Cities

Orientation Divisions:

East 19B		North West 19R
Near East 19C		North 19S
Middle East 19D		North East 19W
Far East 19E		Inside 19X
South East 19F		Outside 19Y
South 19G		
South West 19H		
West 19M		

7.2.2.4 Time Isolates

The term Time Isolate usually denotes millennium/century, decade, year and so on. It also denotes day and night, seasons such as summer and winter, time, meteorological quality such as wet, dry and stormy, etc. Time Isolate is most concrete fundamental category. As the Time facet can occur only in the last round of a subject, there is no need to indicate the round in its names. Zone 1 and 3 are assigned to represent Time Isolate.

Ranganathan has divided Time Isolate in the following two types:

1. Public Time
2. Featured Time

1. **Public Time:** Time conventionally reckoned from the assumed year of birth of Jesus Christ or any other year as origin in public time.

Public time is represented by Roman capitals as the first significant digit. It is attached by a connecting symbol 'Single Connecting Comma (')' in the construction of the Class number.

The schedule of Time Isolate is divided into two parts. Alphabet A to D represent different units of the time while from alphabet E onwards each alphabet represents a century.

1. E32 for 1032 AD
2. M00 for 1800 AD
3. N for 20th Century
4. N5 for 5th decade of the 20th Century
5. N55 for 1955 AD

Making Time Isolate for Before Christ period, the number will be constructed from alphabet B and C. For example, the number for 675 BC is C324 and is derived as under:

999

<u>675</u>

324, i.e. C324

This method of determining the digit of Basic Class (BC) Number may be called 'the method of compliment'.

The alphabet D represents 10,000 years, i.e. the first millennium AD. Hence the period herein would be indicated as follows:

Years	Number
1 AD	D001
10AD	D010
100AD	D100
490AD	D490
999AD	D999

Abhigyan Shakuntalam by Kalidasa 011,1C942,1 (Born in 57 BC).

Ranganathan has divided the period of 100 years in five effective decade as follows:

0—19	is represented by effective decade 1
20—39	is represented by effective decade 3
40—59	is represented by effective decade 5
60—79	is represented by effective decade 7
80—99	is represented by effective decade 9
1960 to 79	N 7

Use of arrows: To show the past or future period in the Time Isolate, Ranganathan suggested the use of arrows. He has confined its use only in Depth Classification and in Documentary Work for specialist readers.

For the past period backward arrow is used ←

For future period forward arrow is used →

Examples

Unemployment Problem in India— From 1961 to 1964: Y:433,44'N64 ← N61

Future of Ayurveda in India: LB.44'N →

2. Featured Time: Sometimes day, night, season, etc. are required to be shown in Time Isolation in addition to or without

Public Time Isolate. Ranganathan has made provision to show this as Time Isolate Level 2 [T2] and named it as featured time. It is represented by Roman smalls as first significant digits. The connecting symbol for featured Time Isolate is also Single Inverted Comma (').

Examples

1. *Snow Period in Kashmir in 1961*: U.4447 'N61 'p 8.

2. *Pilgrimage to Varanasi in Winter Season of 1965*: Q:4198.445213 'N65 'N7.

8

Facet Device (Phase Relation)

If the Decimal Fraction Notation gave hospitality at one point, the concept of facet device provided for hospitality at many points.

— Decimal Fraction Notation — Hospitality at one point
— Facet Device — Hospitality at many points
— Versatility of Decimal Fraction is — 1
— Versatility of facet device is — $1 \times 2 \times 3 \times 4 \times 5 = 120$
  Ratio is 120:1

Example:

D.C. Notation	Facet Device in CC Notation						
5	MC	P	M	E	S	T	
54	2	3	1	5	4	N	step 1
546							
546.3							
546.34	2	36	151	55	421	N63	step 2
546.342							

Literature Explosion
1. Complex Subject
   (a) Basic class
   (b) Between Isolates of facets
   (c) Between sub-isolate of facet isolates

Three levels of phase relation:

(a) Inter-Subject

(b) Intra-Facet

(c) Intra-Array

Phase: It is a part of a complex subject derived from any one main class of knowledge.

Phase Relation: The inter-action of two normally distinct subjects is called Phase Relation.

Complex Subject: The subject is complex, when it represents the interaction of the original subject with separate subject.

Complex Isolate: The isolate is complex when:

(a) It is formed by the combination of two or more isolates in the same facet of a Basic Class.

(b) To express the relation between them.

(c) But when the extension of one of the isolates is restricted without bringing out any relation between them.

Complex Sub-Isolates

Complex sub-isolate is formed by the combination of two or more sub-isolates in the same isolates and same facet of basic class to express relation between them.

First Phase

"The constituent of two phase subject, which is the primary subject of exposition or is otherwise deemed to be primary" is called its First Phase.

Second Phase

"The constituent of two phased specific subject which is merely effective in the exposition of the first phase" is called the Second Phase.

8.1 Types of Phase Relation

While making facet analysed entries, subjects are categorized in two groups:

1. Subjects with Phase Relation.

2. Subjects not involving Phase Relations.

8.1.1 Subject with Phase Relation

Subjects with Phase-Relation is grouped in 6 sub-groups:

(a) General Phase Relation—Pol. Sc. and Eco.—WOaX.

(b) Bias Phase Relation—Economics for Politicians—WObX.

(c) Comparison Phase Relation—Pol. Sc. and Eco compared—WOcX.

(d) Difference Phase Relation—Difference between Pol. & Eco. WOdX.

(e) Influencing Phase Relation—Influence of Eco on Pol. — WOgX.

(a) **General Phase Relation:** When there is phase relation of a more or less general nature or non-descriptive kind, it is known as General Phase Relation.

Class number of small ordinal value will have precedence over the other—WOaX.

(b) **Bias Phase Relation:** When one Phase is biased towards the other phase, it is known as Bias Phase Relation.

Biasing Phase will have precedence over the Biased Phase.

Phase 1   —   Biased Phase

Phase 2   —   Biasing Phase   —WObX

(c) **Comparison Relation:** When the phases are compared with each other, is known as Comparison Phase Relation. The class number having ordinal value will have precedence over the other.

— WOcX

(d) **Difference Phase Relation:** If the difference between the two phases is expounded it is known as Difference Phase Relation.

The class number having smaller ordinal value will have precedence over the other.

(e) **Influencing Relation**: If one phase expounded the influence on the other phase, it is known as Influencing Phase.

Example: Influence on Morphology on Physiology 9 (The isolate influenced will come first) G: 30r2.

8.1.2 Intra-Facet Phase Relation

When the relation exists between the isolates of the same facet, it is known as Intra-Facet Phase Relation. Colon has the following connecting symbols for it:

Connecting Symbols	Type of Relation	Class	No.
Oj	General	Trend in Morphology and Physiology	G:20j3
Ok	Bias	Physiology for Pathologists	G:30k4
Om	Comparison	Morphology & Physiology compared	G:20m3
On	Difference	Difference between Morphology & Physiology	G:20n3
Or	Influence	Influence of Morphology on Physiology	G:30r2

8.1.3 Intra-Array Phase Relation

When the relations exist between the sub-isolate of an Isolate under a facet in a Basic Class, it is known as Intra-Array relation. Colon has following connecting symbols:

Connecting Symbols	Type of Relation	Class	No.
Ot	General	Rural and the City folk culture	Y31Ot5:1
Ou	Bias	City culture for Rural people	Y353u1:1
Ov	Comparison	Powers of Legislative Council of U.P., a comparison V4	
Ow	Difference	Difference between Direct and Representative Democracy	W610w2
Oy	Influence	Influence of City life on Rural life	Y310y5:1

Examples:

Document Reference	Facet Analysis	Class Number Phase I	Phase II
1. Adm. and improvement of reading	Reading Method (BS) Bias to Management (BS). Executive [IPI]	3V	8,2,8
2. Maths for Economists, 1954	Maths (BS) Bias to Economics	B	X
3. Elements of modern Statistics for students of Economics and Business, 1965	Statistics (BS) Bias to Economics (BS)	BT	X
4. Operation Research for Management	Operation Research(BS) Bias to Management	BTT	8
5. Physics for Medical students	Physics (BS) Bias to Medicine(BS)	C	L
6. Introduction to Chemistry for Biology students, 1965	Chemistry Bias to Biology(BS)	E	G
7. Weather Forecasting for Aeronautics	Meteorology(BS) Weather (IPI), Forecast (IMPI) Bias to Aviation (BS)	HV7,1:28,91MD53	

Phase Relation:

1. Sorting: (i) Subjects with Phase Relation (ii) Subject without Phase Relation.

2. Further sorting of subject with phase relation:

(a) General Phase Relation.

(b) Bias Phase Relation.

(c) Comparison Phase Relation.

(d) Difference Phase Relation.

(e) Tool Phase Relation.

(f) Influencing Phase Relation.

Bias Phase Relation

It indicates that the exposition of the subject forming Phase I is biased towards Phase 2.

Sequence of subjects: Phase 1 should be to the subject whose exposition is biased towards the other subject. Phase 1 is called the Biased Phase and Phase 2 the Biasing Phase.

9

Rounds and Levels

Ranganathan subsequently realised that the first three of the Fundamental categories (Personality, Matter and Energy) are liable to occur more than once in any given subject, and this led him to evolve the system of what he calls 'Round and Levels', so as to maintain this order of increasing concreteness.

Example: Shakespeare's *Hamlet* contains four:

Literature.	English	Drama	Shakespeare	Hamlet
mc	P	P2	P3	P4

9.1 Rounds

Round denotes a cyclic recurrence of fundamental categories in the facet analysis of a subject.

Ranganathan assumes that the categories of P, M and E can manifest more than once within a class number. Such reappearances started off by energy facet. The second and the third manifestations of energy in one of the same subject are called "Second Round Energy", Third round Energy and these are characterised as [2E] [3E], etc.

When a particular focus of a subject is considered from the Energy Facet, it becomes imperative to specify various kinds of process of problems. And while specifying the varied type of process or problem, we find the personality facet repeat:

Example:

Broken in	Disease	Blood	Human body
	(Energy)	(Personality)	(Personality)

Second personality facet is the basic class.

So we get medicine in short—[E], [P], [L]

Put in sequence—L (P): [E]

Now let us consider the subject:

Example: A disease of blood of the human body caused by the malarial parasite:

Malarial parasite is new focus.

It is manifestation of personality.

Personality facet is repeated here.

This repeated personality facet exceeds the energy facet.

Now we get the following sequence:

L(P):[E](P)

No doubt this is a violation of principle of decreasing concreteness.

The concept of round comes up as solution of this problem.

The second personality facet is written as (2P).

So it will become L(P):(E)(2P).

Advantage

Analysing the subject in different facets :

(a) A consistent order is maintained.

(b) Gross classification becomes impossible.

(c) If the strict facet formula is strictly followed, the possibility of classifying the same book in two different places cannot arise.

(3P) Third round

(2P) Second round

	Medicine	Disease	Treatment	Inject method
Injection methods for the treatment	MC	E	2E	3P

J581:75:5 Cleaning of groundnut leaves.

J311:438:55 (G) Biological concept of the insect pest.

KZ31:73:97 The use of butter.

In other words, the personality facet may manifest immediately after the first round of the energy facet (E). This is termed as the second round personality [2P]. The second round of energy facet [2E] gives third round of the personality [3P] and so on. This however, needs many connecting symbols for its occurrence. In some cases, the second round personality may have divisions into level personality [2P2]. This needs a connecting symbol comma (,) and can be put after the first round energy facet. This facet [2P1] is freely used in the main classes Chemistry and Education.

Y33:4353:67.4473 'N64 famine relief work in urban areas of Bihar 1964.

9.2 Levels

The concept of whole personality spreads into a number of levels. These levels are termed as [P1] [P2] [P3] [P4]. According to Dr. Ranganathan personality may manifest itself in a subject more than once in two or more levels. These levels of the fundamental category 'Personality' are indicative of the whole part, portion, organ and constituent.

The existence of levels in a personality can be indicated by taking a few illustrations.

In the main class Literature, the personality facet deals with language. This, however, has to be divided according to different characteristics of form, author and work. All these can be enumerated within the personality facet and can be termed as levels of personality: 'Form' as second level [P2], "Author" as third level [P3], and 'Work' as fourth level [P4]. Similarly in the main class Political Science, the personality facet deals with the type of government. The organs of the government are enumerated in the second level [P2]. The connecting symbol for the various levels of personality is comma (,).

In other words, within the Personality facet, we find a number of levels into which the whole personality is spread. These are known as levels of personality facet. P1, P2, P3, P4 and so on.

These different levels are arranged with the help of principles of helpful sequence. The systems and the specials are also considered a manifestation of personality and because of their wider jurisdiction they precede other levels of the facet.

Main Class	DC No.	Personality Facet	CC No.
Psychology	132	Abnormal Psychology	56
Economics	336	Public Finance	X7
Chemistry	546	Inorganic Chemistry	E1
Zoology	596	Vertebrates	K9

Levels of Personality

Main class	P1	P2	P3	P4
Literature	Language	Form	Author	His work

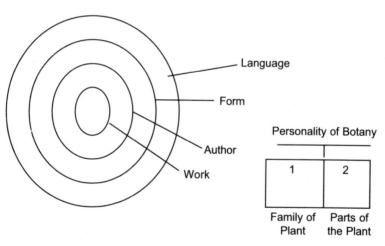

Personality of Botany

1	2
Family of Plant	Parts of the Plant

Language	1st level	— Personality
Form	2nd level	— Personality
Author	3rd level	— Personality
Work	4th level	— Personality

0[P], [P2], [P3], [P4]

= NA 44, j6, 45:5

    P   P2   P3

Mughal architecture of the museum
Pillars : a section

NA 441, G37,45:8 Model of castle pillars in Pallava architecture

| | E | P3 | P4 | P | | P2 |

NB 52, D5, 691:3 Roman style of city theatre : A plan

| | P | P2 | | P3 | P4 | E |

0152, 1M84, 16 Saket – Maithili Sharan Gupta (Born in 1884, 6th book)

| | P | P2 | P3 |

Z(Q6), 985:2 Execution of the Negotiable Instrument in Christian Law

| | E | | E2 | | P |

Z, A 75,5 Trial of war-criminals

| | P3 | | P2 |

10

Devices

Colon classification scheme provides certain standards, rules for the construction of class numbers.

There is a need for the minuteness of classification in most of the subjects, so that all the sources of libraries on every specific subjects are enclosed to the reader.

Dr. Ranganathan made colon classification more hospitable, i.e. hospitability — both in arrays and chains — with the help of various devices. They are often used for the sub-divisions of many classes. These devices are:

1. Chronological Device.
2. Geographical Device.
3. Subject Device.
4. Super Imposition Device.
5. Mnemonic Device.
6. Alphabetical Device.

10.1 Chronological Device

A chronological device consists of using the appropriate chronological number for the further sub-division of a class which is capable of chronological division.

The chronological device has been used for the formation or the sub-division of an isolate which is capable of chronological formation of sub-division or when the individualisation of the isolate or sub-isolates may be made to depend conveniently on the period of origin or birth or on the year of first invention or on the year of discovery or on the year of initiation or commencement or on the year of occurance or on the year that may be definitely associated with the respective isolate in any manner or for any reason.

Some of the cases where this device may be employed are generally indicated either in the schedules or in the rules. Similar cases, where it may be employed, will suggest themselves in the course of actual classification.

Example: Shakespeare's *Hamlet*   0111, 2J64, 51

J64 used as personality to fix the author number and is denoted by chronological device by taking the year of birth of the author.

2:51 N3	— Colon classification 1933
SN	Gestalt Psychology (Initiated in 1907) (1900 by Max Werthimer) Century as it is first in 20th century
SN1	— Behaviouristic Psychology (Founded) In 1912 by H. John Bradus Up to two digits (century and latest effected decade)
SN14	— Individualistic Psychology (Estd. in 1914 by Alfred Adler)
C 84 N01	— Quantam Theory (in 1901)
015 : 2D40	— Kalidas
0:2 M 56	— Bernard Shaw (Born in 1856)
N	20th century (1900-1999AD)
N3	1930
N54	1954

10.2 Geographical Device

Colon classification provides schedule of Geographical divisions from page 2.8 to 2.17. It helps us to secure parallel sequences of classes of all geographical arrays, wherever they may occur.

With the use of geographical divisions, a Geographical Device (GD) has been evolved to use the appropriate number, i.e. continent, country, state, districts, etc. to individualise the isolates and sub-isolates on the basis of place.

This device is generally used whenever directed either in the schedule or in the rules.

There is no common geographical divisions; instead there are four methods of geographical sub-divisions.

(a) **Community in history and law:** By a series of numbers assigned to a place in the regular sequence of the notation, e.g. SH Angling, SH 603-643 to Europe; SH 651-667 to Asia.

There is no number building device for geographical sub-divisions. Here, place is divided in some detail specially the continent.

(b) By leaving a set of numbers blank and referring to a special table where countries are listed with numbers that fill the blanks, e.g.

H × 650 Socialism, Communism and Anarchism

H × 651-680 By country table V Geographical number for Mexico is 11

H × 661 is Communism in Mexico

H × 840 is Anarchism

H × 851 is Anarchism in Mexico

(c) By decimal numbers this is very similar to the 4th method discussed below:

Class G Geography table 1

.69	Asia	.43	Great Britain
.7	China	.44	England
.71	India & Cylone	.45	Scotland
.72	Indo-China		

(d) By Alphabetical sub-divisions by country A-Z, e.g. DA 662 Castles, Halls, Cathedrals, etc.

SH 101.FS Fish Culture in Finland

Example=   Functions of Indian Prime Minister up to 1960—
                V44,21:3 'N7

Analysis-   V   History
             V44   History of India
             V44,21   Indian Prime Minister
             V44,21:3   Functions of Indian Prime Minister
             V44,21:3 'N7   Functions of Indian Prime Minister
                                  brought up to 1960's

Here, V44 is obtained by Geographical device.

10.3 Subject Device

The number of isolates in an array of any order is unlimited; unlimited in the sense of the term. Due to the result of growing specialisation on minor subjects, it becomes difficult to provide a permanent place to isolate or sub-isolate under every main class. Only those isolates are given a permanent place in one or more main classes on which sufficient literature has accumulated. In this case the isolate idea enumerated in one main class is borrowed and used in another class.

The subject device consists of using the appropriate class numbers for the formation or sub-divisions of a class which is capable of such formation or sub-division. It is claimed that by this device any number of co-ordinate classes can be accommodated in any array. The classes where this device is applied are generally indicated either in the schedules or in rules, e.g., in useful Arts (M). We find instructions for further divisions by subject device.

M (B1)   Calculating Machine

M   —   Useful Art

B1   —   Mathematics (Borrowed from other class)

( )   —   Sign of subject device

In simple words, subject device is temporarily occurrence of an isolate of a class under a different class. It is enclosed in circular bracket.

Wherever this device is used isolates are generally indicated either in the schedules or in the rules.

Colon classification uses subject device to individualisation.

1. Some substances in Organic Chemistry.
2. Some buildings in Architecture.
3. Some subjects in Sculpture.
4. Special views in Metaphysics.
5. Subjects in teaching techniques.
6. Industries in Economics.
7. Some other places as directed in schedule.

    D66,8 (M7)   Textile Machinery

    Z (Q2)   Hindu Law

In other words, there is need to accommodate any isolate in an array. This is commonly dominant in the documents. The notation should be equipped to translate it whenever the need arises.

DC   — 'Divide like 000 – 999 at number of places.

CC   — The method applied is subject device.

The isolate number is put in bracket along with its main class number, and attached to the main class where it occurs.

Example: Psychology of University Teachers   S4 (T4)

              Hindu Ethics   R4 (Q2)

              Industrial Microbiology   F: (G91)

This device also provides hospitability in array, order of such arrays where temporary occurrence and order of such arrays where temporary occurrence takes place mostly in lower orders of arrays.

(a) Form of isolate to take the help of other main class. It is used in two ways:

To sharpen an already existing isolate	To form an isolate
Business library of Physics = 24	There are several business libraries and other libraries based on (SD) subject device.

2 library

4 Business library by (SD)

24 (C) — Physics library—In sharpening of an already existing isolate, but you do not find any enumeration schedule. It will be sub-divided further. Hence, no connecting symbols.

(b) To form an Isolate—New isolate appears, which cannot be taken as sub-division.

Further Analysis: Facet of time, energy or other. This is energy facet. No readymade number but should be accommodated under energy. It will be from subject device.

Example: Application of Statistical methods of Library Science.

1. Facet — Statistics (E)

   2: (B28) = Statistics in library

2. Teaching of Mathematics in higher secondary school = T2:3 (B)

   — Subject device has been instructed in (2P) in Education schedule.

3. Sulphar Metabolism = G:33 ; (E161)

4. Automation in libraries = 2: (D65,8(B))

   Automation (E) – There is no number in schedule in Engineering.

   D 678 – Servomechanism. It may be related with it. There is gap between 74-78. That is 75, 76, 77.
   More we may use seminal mnemonics.
   Rule part of Mnemonics.
   Digit 7. Integrated personality.

Subject Device in Idea plane

Temporary occurrence

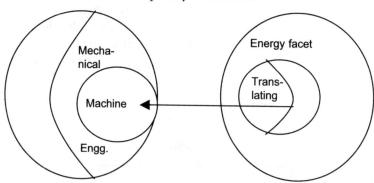

Main class engineering borrowed the isolate idea from the main class linguistics, to form his specific subject:

Agricultural Law   –   J, (Z) – As P

Agricultural Microfilm –   J; (2,151) – As M

Agricultural Analysis   –   J: (E:3) – As E

10.4 Super Imposition Device

Super imposition means imposing or putting a thing on some thing else.

Super imposition device (SID) consists of –

(a) Attaching to one number within a facet, another numbers within the same facet.

(b) With distinctive connecting symbol chosen for the purpose.

Two facets, which are represented separately in the schedule, are represented by joining them with the connecting symbol hyphen (-)

Urban Youth   — Y12-33

Veins of Arms   — L163-36

Sequence: An intelligible sequence between the isolate should be maintained.

— British possession in Africa — V6-56

— African possession in Britain – V56-6 – not correct Hence V6-56 is right.

In other words, when two separately scheduled isolates enumerated in an array appear in a specific, one subordinate to another, it is said to be super-imposition situation.

This happens when there is a mutual denudation between two isolates in a facet.

Suppose a specific subject like "History of Portuguese Africa" is to be individualised. The position will be as follows:

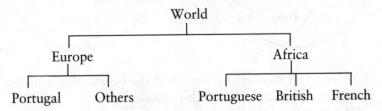

When we say 'Portuguese Africa' – Class Africa to subdivided by Portugal, an isolate under Europe.

Specific Subjects	Translation in colon
History – Africa — Portugal	V6-42
History – Africa — Britain	V6-56
History – Africa — France	V6-53

1. Connecting symbol – '- ' Hyphen.
2. Intelligible sequence between the isolates should be maintained.
3. Follow hospitality in chain in notation.

10.5 Mnemonics Device

This device is also a canon which falls under the area of notation.

It has bearing on entire scheme of classification.

It is a general canon.

According to the canon a particular digit should represent the same and similar ideas under different main classes where they occur.

Bliss says "Notation as a kind of symbolic language depend extremely on memory of meanings."

The term Mnemonic means "an aid to memory". The notation should be used in such a manner that similar idea gets the similar number. This will be an aid to memory.

Mnemonic Device (MD) is also used for making further divisions of class. Ranganathan name the Mnemonics as Seminal Mnemonics. The one and the some digit is used to represent the seminally equivalent entities irrespective of their occurrence in any main class. But these terms of mnemonics are used differently in different main classes.

Digit 1 is used for Unity, God, World, the first in evolution or time, one dimension or line, solid state, and all other entities.

Digit 2 is used as Mnemonics for two dimensions, plane, comics, form, structure, anatomy, morphology, sources of knowledge, physiography, constitution physical anthropology and all other entities.

Digit 3 is used as Mnemonics for three dimensions, space, cubios, analysis, function, physiology, syntax, method, social anthropology and other related entities.

Digit 4 is used as Mnemonics for heat, pathology, disease, transport, interlinking, synthesis, hybrid, salt and other entities.

Digit 5 is used as Mnemonics for energy, light, radiation organic, liquid, water, ocean, foreign land, alien, external, environment, ecology, public controlled plan, emotion, foliage, aesthetics, women, sex, comic and other related entities.

Digit 6 is used as Mnemonics for dimensions, subtle, mysticism, money, finance, abnormal, phylogeny, evolution and other entities.

Digit 7 is used as Mnemonics for personality, ontogeny, integrated, Holism, value, public finance and other related entities.

Digit 8 is used as Mnemonics for travel, organisation, fitness.

Mnemonics is the use of symbols in such manner that they have a more or less constant meaning (occurrence) when applied anywhere in the scheme.

Example: Form division or common sub-divisions in D.C. 1-9 and their value is constant.

-03 – dictionary .05 periodicals.

Bliss: Mnemonic effect was achieved with his interior divisions which have constant value.

Brown: Achieved the same effect with his category number, which includes form divisions.

L.C.: It lacks form divisions.

There are three types of Mnemonics:

1. Verbal Mnemonics (Literal Mnemonics)
2. Schedule Mnemonics (Systematic Mnemonics)
3. Seminal Mnemonics

10.5.1 Verbal Mnemonics (Literal Mnemonics)

Means

(a) Alphabets used in a notation may also be taken to represent the words.

(b) The first alphabet of the work will stand for the entire word.

U stands for useful art.

C stands for Chemistry.

There are Verbal Mnemonics.

In CC verbal Mnemonics are not used if a sequence is more helpful and of logical systematic order.

Alphabetical device may be used as last resort. DC, CC-alphabetical device has been used rarely.

L.T.   T is used for Technology.

B.C.   C is used for Chemistry.

Needham— Verbal (literal) Mnemonics should be incidental.

10.5.2 Systematic Mnemonics (Scheduled Mnemonics)

Scheduled mnemonics demand that similar digits should be

assigned to similar classes and terms, if they occur under more than one class.

The mnemonics which are employed in a consistent manner in notation are called Systematic Mnemonics. Such mnemonics are forms, sub-divisions, linguistics and geographical number etc., because their value is constant. For this reason, systematic mnemonics are also called "Constant Mnemonics".

There are four kinds of scheduled mnemonics:

(a) Common Isolate.

(b) Isolate or sub-division of isolates got by subject devices.

(c) Isolate pertaining two or few basic classes running parallel.

(d) Isolate with casual mnemonics.

(a) **Common Isolates:** It is a isolate idea denoted by the same isolate term and represented by the same isolate number whatever be the host class to which it is attached.

CC– (C1) – attachable to many classes, not all.

DC– Form Division– used with the subject when applicable

— AC1 (Applicable after space facet)	2
— AC1 (Applicable after time facet)	10
— Posturiorising energy common isolates (EC1)	12
— Posturiorising personality common isolate (ACI)	14
— Posturiorising matter common isolate (MC1)	471
— Time isolate (T1) – level 1	31
(T1) – level 2	12
— Space isolate (S1) – level 1	1440
(S1) – level 2	10
— Anteriorisiong common isolate (ACI) (Applicable before space facet)	18
	2020

(b) **Isolate by Subject Device:** CC defines subject device as:

The subject device consists in using the appropriate class characteristics for the information or the sub-division of an isolate which is capable of such information or sub-division or when the individualisation of the isolates, or sub-isolates may be made to depend conveniently on a class that may be definitely associated with the respective foci in any manner or for any reason.

(c) **Parallel Schedules of Isolates:** Certain characteristics recur as the basis for the information of any array of some order or other of several classes. It will be help to memory if the isolates in each array of such a set occur in a sequence parallel to those in every other array of the same set and in addition the same isolate number of digits is used to represent the corresponding isolates in all the arrays conformity to this is demanded by the canon of scheduled mnemonics.

(1) DC Mnemonics   —   DC   CC
    Literature authors   821.64   0:1L28
    Oliver Goldsmith as part
    Literature author   824.66   06 6L28
    Oliver Goldsmith as essayist

(2) Cereals   —
    Farming of cereals   633.1   J38
    Adulteration of cereals   614.312   L:523:338
    Diet of cereals   612.39273   L:533:338

(3) Transport   —
    Air transport service   629.1382   43
    Transport in mines   622.6   D3:4
    Transport in goods   658.7885   9:4

(4) Facet device   —
    Gall bladder   L292
    Anatomy of gall bladder   L292:2
    Inflammation   L415
    Inflammation of eyes   L183:415
    Inflammation of kidneys   L51:415

(5) Geographical Device   —
    Flora of India   1:12.44
    Fonna of India   K:12.44
    Psychology of Indians   S7444
    Geography of India   U44
    History of India   V44

(6) Chronological Device   —
    Chesterton as poet   0–, 1 M74
    Chesterton as a dramatist   0–, 2 M74
    Chesterton as a Novelist   0–, 3 M74
    Chesterton as a prose writer   0–, 6 M74

(7) Subject device   —
    X-rays diagnosis   L:4:40253
    X-ray therapy   L:4 : 6253
    Making X-ray apparatus   MC 53

(8) Phase device   —
    Psychology   S
    Maths for Psychology   B0bs
    Statistics for Psychology   B280 bs

(d) **Isolate with Casual Mnemonics:** Scheduled with casual mnemonics differ from scheduled mnemonic in that only a few isolates in the array correspond with one another instead of all the isolate. Here is a list of such casual mnemonics:

B13 [E] only 1, 2, 3 and 6 and parallel to the canonical divisions of B mathematics.

B6 [E] Only 1, 2, 3 and 6 are parallel to the canonical divisions of b mathematics.

S [P] only 1 to 7 correspond to 1 to 7 of [P] of T.

Y [P] only 1 to 8 correspond to 1 to 8 of [P2] of Z law.

10.5.3 Seminal Mnemonics

The Seminal Mnemonics has been used with respect of Indo-Arabic numerals only. It is rather impossible to denote by any unique and absolute term of a natural language the seminal idea respected by each of the eight Indo-Arabic numerals omitting 9, which has been treated as a sectorising empty digit in CC.

The following is the representation of such a pattern arranged in their spectral scatter of the seminal idea.

Example:

Mnemonic significance of digit 1.

Unity– First in evolution

God – One dimension

World – Solid state

In the same way up to digit 8.

(a) **In energy facet:** The highest percentage of seminal mnemonics occurs in energy facet. The naturalness of this will be appreciated. It a remembered that Ranganathan is intuitive hit on seminal mnemonics first occurred only respect of [E].

Secondly the incidence of seminal mnemonics is as much as 93% in [2E]. Higher the round and near the seminal level.

(b) **In personality facet:** The number array isolates is largest in [P] indeed. It forms 90% of the total number of array isolate in CC. Personality facet will grow in number and in facet it will keep growing even after energy and matter isolates reach very near their limit of growth.

Example:

3 Function	Pol. Sc.
3 Physiology	Bio. Science
3 Social Activities	Sociology
2 Constitution	Pol. Sc.
2 Morphology	Bio. Sc.
2 Phy. Anthropology	Sociology
3 Disease	Bio. Sc.
3 Soc. Pathology	Soc. Sc.
3 Tort	Law
5 Fundamentals	Physics
5 Logic	Philosophy
5 Description	Useful Art

Connecting Symbols— Indicating digits connecting symbols also stand for ideas:

: energy

; matter
, personality.

10.6. Alphabetical Device

When we fail to divide or sharpen any isolate with the help of other devices, then the last resort is to use the alphabetical device.

Alphabetical device consists in using the first or the first two or the first three, etc. initial letters (all in capital) of the name of the entity, existential or conceptual for the formation or the sub-division of the isolate. It secures helpful sequences. This device is applied in case of proper names, trade names, which are internationally accepted.

The following convention is suggested to deal with the names having the same initial letters:

First letter — Used for most favoured entity having greatest literary warrant or which is the first on which literature arrives.

First two letters — Used for second favoured entity with the same initial letter using 'favoured' in the above sense.

First three letters — May be invoked if the name of another entity has the same two initial letters as the one already selected for two letter representation.

This device is used only in cases where no other method of sub-division gives more helpful sequence.

Example—	Hero Cycle	D5125H
	Basmati Rice	J381B
	Dasehari Mango	J3751D
[S2] Facet isolates		
	Birds of Himalayas	K96: 12.4.g7H
	Travels in Udaipur	U8.4437, U
Generalia		
	Gandhiana	z G
	Nehruana	z N
	Bibliography of Hindi	a 3152, 3S
	book published by S. Chand	

11

Systems and Specials

11.1 Systems

The term school of thought or system indicates that a particular subject has been viewed from different approaches. The number of systems will be equal to the number of approaches and under each approach the whole range of the subject is treated, e.g.

Under Education: Montessori approach

Under Economics: Marxist approach

Under Psychology: Through concept of psycho-analysis.

These examples reveal that under different subjects, the entire area can be examined from the point of view of established schools of thought or systems.

Definition: According to Ranganathan, the term system still evades or clear-cut definition and therefore, he takes it to be an assumed term, in depth classification.

"An exposition of a subject can only be according to some system. In other words, there can be no document on a basic class, Quasi Basic class."

By this system of Ranganathan it becomes obligatory that the exposition of a subject should be according to some system. He also feels that the concept of system is intrinsic to the Universe of Knowledge itself. This means that systems and system facets exist in the idea plane. The canon of helpful sequence will demand that all the documents according to a particular system should be placed together.

Systems of a basic class are distinguished from one another by the chronological device; the chronological number is added to the basic class number. The epoch used is the year chosen as the one in which the system was first expounded normally a subject in universe of knowledge, which is recognised in a main class, belongs to a particular school of thought.

Subject pertaining to a school of the thought has given rise to the literature on it. This is called by the term literary warrant. In fact the demarcation in to the universe of knowledge in certain broad divisions and classes are based on principles of literary warrant. Many of the main classes in any scheme of classification are recognised on the basis of this principle of canonical or traditional class.

In certain situation, a subject may not belong to one school of thought. It may develop through a school of thought along with other school of thought. It is of course too difficult to get the exact year, and even historical research into this problem may not be able to assert a particular year. But systems are not invented every year or even every decade, so it is sufficient if approximately century is represented in a class number. Indeed in regard to the ancient Indian systems of medicine, Ayurveda and even the country could not be asserted. The chronological numbers shown against them in the above schedule are therefore, simply those representing two of the divisions of the pre-Christian era.

Viewed as a class, a system is called on Amplified (enlarged) basic class. The chronological isolates, attached to a basic class to denote systems are said to constitute an Amplifying facet. We may also state that:

Basic class + Amplified class = Amplified basic class = Idea plane.

Basic class number + Amplified isolate number = Amplified basic class number (Notational plane).

LB – Amplified (enlarged) Basic class

L(B) – Amplified facet

Analysis of system

1. Recognition of system was not enough.
2. It is necessary to find out as to which facet of a Basic class it belongs?

CC has five categories: One is to be selected out of them (Time, Personality, Space, Energy and Matter) because their different jurisdictions cannot accommodate it. Therefore, it was deemed to be a manifestation of personality. Personality found it convenient to allot to it its first round.

As the levels of this round of Personality were already occupied in the second zone, i.e. Arabic number, they were analysed by symbols of the first zone, i.e. Lower case letters which gave them a place interior to symbols of the second zone.

Example:

Idea Analysis	BC	1 Pa	1P1	E
Term Analysis	Main class	System	Personality	Energy
Kernels	Medicine	Homeopathy	Digestive System	Disease
Numbers	L	L	2	4
Connecting : Symbols		Not needed	,	
Synthesis		L L , 2:4		

11.1.1 Notational Provisions

These findings in the idea plane were to be provided form in the notation of a scheme. Along with the systems, Ranganathan also recognised Branch Systems and specials. All these were accommodated under personality in first round. As the second one was already occupied by the traditional levels of first round personality, new findings got the first zone for their symbolisation in the following manner:

Example:

Personality

First Zone			Second Zone			
1Pa	1Pb	1Pc	1P1	1P2	1P3	1P4

When new findings were placed under the first zone of personality, the following rules were adopted of the personality facet.

(a) The system level should precede all other levels of the personality facet.

(b) The special level should succeed the system level but it should precede the rest of the levels of personality facet.

(c) If the system, special and personality isolate, each should be used to connect special and personality isolate numbers. If only special and personality isolate numbers appear, a comma should not be used before the personality Isolate number. It need not be used to connect it, as is the general practice. Example—

(i) LL, 9C, 2

(ii) L9C, 2

(iii) L2

11.1.2 Favoured System

One system out of all systems, will have the highest literary warrant at a particular point of time.

The source of this assumption appears to be the present day supremacy of allopathy (in literary warrant) over other systems of medicine. This meant that one system in each class will be favoured system. Therefore the favoured system was identified with the basic class number itself.

In Medicine, Allopathy is not enumerated under system. The main class number L itself stands for it. All documents from allopathy point of view are accommodated under the main class number. The result is that the books on allopathy precede the books on other systems in their arrangement.

An exposition of a subject will have to be according to some system. In other words, there can be no document in a basic class que. The idea in a basic class are: Superior (ineffable), unless it is amplified to represent a system. In the Notational plane, this means that no documentation can have an unamplified Basic Class number to begin its class number. However, in practice, one of the systems of Basic class is taken as a favoured system.

The favoured system is determined by literary warrant, or rather, by the current tendency in literary warrant. Allopathy, for example, is taken as the favoured system in medicine. To satisfy the law of parsimony, the amplifying facet is omitted in the class number of the favoured system. If a document deals disjunctively with many systems, its basic class number is amplified by the digit A.

11.1.3 Non-Favoured System

All the facets which can be added to the favoured system may be added to a non-favoured system also. Generally, the same schedules of the various facets may be suitable for use in the favoured system as well as in the other systems, but it is not obligatory. Each system may call for a different schedule with different isolates in one or more facets. These may have to be worked out separately for each system. To make depth classification efficient in the service of micro thought, such differing schedules may be needed. This is the piece of work and yet remains to be done. Intensive progress in the ancient history of the subject will produce documents making this piece of work urgent. Ancient chemistry, usually referred to as alchemy, may need problem schedules different from those of modern chemistry. So also Ayurveda may need at least a few extra problem divisions.

Example:

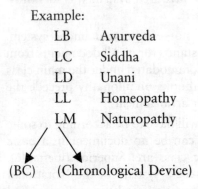

LB	Ayurveda
LC	Siddha
LD	Unani
LL	Homeopathy
LM	Naturopathy

(BC)   (Chronological Device)

11.1.4 Numbering of Systems

All the system isolates, excluding the favoured system, in a basic class are given the Notational digits according to the Chronological Device. The time of the origin of the system is the characteristic used of it.

For example, in Economics:

XB War Economics (Originated between 9999 to 1000 BC)

XM Cooperative (Originated in the 19th century)

XN16 Syndicalism (Originated in 1916)

XN17 Communism (Originated in 1917).

Systems are not the certain of CC. They exist in the Universe of knowledge. DC and UDC, both recognise them in their notation. There, they are enumerated in a disconnected manner in the schedules. CC has consciously recognised the system facet and has given certain schedules of systems. The result is that all documents on a system can be put together.

11.2 Specials

Specials of a basic class are those isolates under which people specialised. Under them, the entire subject is viewed form the point of view of the field of specialisation. Each subjects came in greater prominence about 50 years ago. Ranganathan analysed that the specials signify restriction on the field of exposition of a subject to a particular range. CC has enumerated a list of specials under different classes, for example:

In Medicine	In Physics
L 9 A Special	C 9 A Specials
L 9 C Child	C 9 B1 Molecular ray
L 9 E Old age	C 9 B2 Atom
L 9 F Female	C 9 D1 Low temperature
L 9 H Tropical	C 9 D8 High temperature,
L 9 T Aviation	etc.
L 9 V War	
L 9 X Industrial	

Each special division mentioned above views the subject from its own angle and covers the entire area as a specialist's concern. A specialist on child medicine will be interested in the study of all organs [P] of the children's body, and all the problems [E]. He will not be equally interested in the organs [P] and problems [E] of old age or female medicine and *vice versa*. The canon of helpful sequence demands that all documents on a specialised area should be put together. To do so, CC adopted them in the penultimate sector of zone 3 and enumerated them with the help of the digits, from 9A to 9Z.

The Roman capitals were allotted to the special isolates in an enumerative manner. The place value of specials was assigned after the systems and therefore the PMEST of a basic class are available for use as sub-divisions of the special.

Example

L 9 C, 2   Digestive system of children

L 9 C : 4   Disease of children

LL, 9C, 2: 4: 6 — treatment of the disease of digestive organs of children according to Homeopathy.

In specials, there is restrictions in the Universe of the basic class. Specials arises out of such a restriction, unlike systems which arise from differences in hypothesis, postulates etc.

For examples: In medicine, child medicine and old age medicine strict the universe of living body of men to that of one within certain age limits. The field of study of each of these is confined to those problems that are peculiar to the restricted age group concerned. Similarly, industrial medicine denotes the study of the medical problems particularly incident to industrial workers. So, also aviation medicine stands for the study of medical problem peculiar to flying, usually at speeds far in access of the one normally experienced in motion on surface and usually at high attitudes with centrifugal accelerations, atmospherical bumps and so on. Specials in Physics would mean the study in physical phenomena, such as properties of matter, electrical conductivity and every problem, when some of the factors are abnormal, such as high pressure, low temperature, high voltage, infinite simulate dimensions, astronomical dimensions and so on. In agriculture, soilless cultivation, dry cultivation, Arctic cultivation, etc. are specials, with abnormal restrictions in soil, water supply, temperature, etc.

Idea Plane: The possibility of such specials was not foreseen thirty years ago when the CC was designed, because in those days there were few books on such specials coming into our experience. But the universe of micro thought, met with in documentations, brings them up fairly often. There was at first difficulty in idea plane itself. In 1957 the literature on each special was kept together to satisfy the canon of helpful sequence. The canon of filiatory sequence requires that documents on a special, i.e. embodying results of study within an abnormal or restricted range of some of the factors should not be mixed up with the documents of some other specials or of any normal system, favoured or not. This means that as each system creates a parallel sequence within a basic class, each special also will create a parallel sequence of its own.

Notational Plane: The indication of idea plane were utilised in the Notational plane. Specials are also individualised by the device of amplification. Amplification really amounts to accommodations in Zone 3. The last octave of Zone 3 having been reserved for systems, it was easily decided that specials should be accommodated in the penultimate octave of Zone 3. The next problem was the choice of the device for getting the first significant digit in the number of the special which can be either by alphabetical device or by chronological device. The specials did not always have an internationally accepted standard names and therefore alphabetical device was not available but it is not easy to determine the year of the beginning of each special. Moreover, it is only in recent years that research has been intensified sufficiently and therefore a crap of specials come up more or less at the same time. For all these reasons, chronological device also had to be abandoned. Finally, we had to land on enumeration, with Roman capitals as base.

In medicine the first four specials have been numbered on the basis of verbal Mnemonics, while last three have been numbered on the basis of scheduled mnemonics in an oblique form, It is not however a subject device.

Special features

1. It is useful for knowledge classification.
2. CC treats them wider than isolates and facets.
3. They are like quasi-basic class.
4. All the facets and their isolates are available for such division under a special and systems.
5. They are also available under basic class.
6. CC calls them amplified basic class of kind one and kind two.
7. Specials exist on individual isolates.

Example: 3A system by (CD) under isolate distribution of [E] in (BC) economics.

Table for Indicator Digit

Sl. No.	Indicator Digit	Name	Significance	Example	Class No.
1	←	Backward arrow	To connect to end point of time	Library science in India from 1947-1974	2.44'N74-'N47
2	→	Forward arrow	To indicate future time	Future of Lib. Sc. in India	2.44'N
3	0	Zero	To indicate future time	Mathematics for engineers	B0b
4	'	Single inverted comma	To indicate time facet	Lib. Sc. in India during 70	2.44'N7
5	.	Dot	To indicate space facet	Library Sc. in India	2.44
6	:	Colon	To indicate energy facet	Classification in libraries	2:51
7	;	Semicolon	To indicate matter facet	Classification of books in public libraries	22; 43:51
8	,	Comma	To indicate personality facet	English poetry	0111, 1
9	-	Hyphen	To indicate super imposition	Divisional Insurance libraries	216-4(x81)

In addition to the above nine connecting symbols, Ranganathan has proposed the following indicator digits for the forthcoming edition of colon classification:

1	=	Equal to	To connect abbreviation in alphabetical device	Merchant of Venice	0111, 2J64 M=N
2	&	Ampersand	To indicate	Econometry Phase Relation	X&e B28

12

Notation

Notation is a system of sign or symbols coined for a specific purpose for classification of knowledge embodied in documents. It has been clear that the entities in knowledge are given names or assigned terms in a natural language; the terms are translated into notations, which is an artificial language.

Ranganathan defines notation as a system of ordinal numbers used to represent the classes in a scheme of classification.

Bliss defines notation as of a system of marks of symbols in some order denoting terms and numbers of a series of system of things.

Mann gives a very short definition: "The symbol which stands for the classes and their sub-divisions is called the notation of that scheme." She says, "A book notation is a shorthand sign standing for the name of the term and forming a convenient means of reference to the arrangement of our classification."

1. Notations are addition to any classification schedule.

2. Notations should in no manner determine the logic, scope or development of classification.

Sayers: "A notation is a series of symbols or shorthand signs. Perhaps 'short signs' would be more accurate — for the terms of classification— and which in their arrangement of classification."

Palmer and Wells define: "Notation as a device for mechanising arrangement and must be composed of written symbols whose order is defined."

Phillips: "A notation is a series of symbols which stands for the names of a class or any division or sub-division of a class and forms a convenient means of reference to the arrangement of a classification."

In view of all definitions it can be defined that notations are signs and symbols which represent the classes, divisions and for the style of writing, and denote their order in the arrangement on the shelves without naming them. Notations also specify the characteristics of the classes from general to specific placing.

Need and function of notation: The terms used in classification of knowledge are to be translated into ordinal numbers, reveals the basic need of notation.

1. Notation is required to replace the terms. It becomes a permanent symbol through which the terms of classification are referred to.

2. It is a medium of and guide to the sequence of terms and fixes their relative position.

   Example: Maths 510 Astronomy 520

3. Alphabetical index is possible only through notation in a classification scheme.

4. It is written on various parts of documents and cards, etc.

5. It helps in the arrangement of documents on the shelves and the entries in the catalogue.

6. Efficient working of the catalogue is dependent on notation.

7. It figures among the guides used in a library.

8. It shows the sequence and subordination and coordination of classes.

9. It shows various types of phase relations between classes, facets, isolates, etc. and differentiates between the facets of a class and between the types of relations.

10. It arranges entries in bibliographies and lists, etc.

11. It restores the sequence of documents, if they are pulled out from their respective places.

12. One can determine the specific subject through notation without reading the text.

13. Notation facilitates the use of mnemonics.

14. It is used for author marks, book numbers and sequence numbers, etc.

15. It is used for charging and discharging of documents.

16. Notation mechanically maintains the sequence of subjects.

Types of Notation: According to Bradley the notation is of two types:

1. Pure Notation.

2. Mixed Notation.

12.1 Pure Notation

If it is one kind of notation that is denoted by forward sequence. It is called pure notation.

Example =

(a) 1 2 3 4 5 6 7 8 9

Or

(b) A B C D E F G H I J K L M N O P Q R S T U V W X Y Z

12.2 Mixed Notation

If more than one kind of symbol is used, it is called mixed notation.

Example:

1 2 3 4 5 6 7 8 9 and A B C D E F G H I J K L M N O P Q R S T U V W X Y Z AND , ; : . ' – and a b c d e f g h i j k l m n o p q r s t u v w x y z and others.

DC: It used pure notation (figures).

Cutter Experiensive Classification used pure notation – letters. Ranganathan used mixed notation in colon classification.

12.3 Qualities of Notation

1. Notations make a good scheme of classification.

2. They lead the determination to perform in order for good scheme of classification.

3. They individualise each document.

4. Notation should be versatile for their convenient use.

5. They are equal for each feature of knowledge to establish their places.

6. They are simple in nature and are commonly known.

According to Sayers, notation has the following qualities:

(a) Bravity in character.

(b) Simplicity in character.

(c) Flexibility in character.

(d) Mnemonic in character.

According to Bliss, it should have the following qualities:

(a) Expansiveness.

(b) Adjustability.

(c) Coordinationship.

(d) Feasibility (meaningfulness).

(e) Simplicity.

General qualities:

(a) Easy to write.

(b) Easy to remember.

(c) More commonly used.

(d) Easy to communicate.

(e) Capacity to reveal the feature, formations and exposition of knowledge.

Ranganathan enumerates the following qualities:

(a) It should be hospitable to new topics in its arrays and chains.

(b) Synthesis should be possible in it.

(c) Its length should be relative to the depth of the class it represents.

(d) It should work as mnemonic in its structure.

Notation has flexibility. It never allows exhaustiveness in a classification scheme as it accommodates all relative classes in array and chain in the schedule, without locating the sequence of either the notation or the classification itself. New subjects include compounds which are made up of elements that are already in the classification by extrapolation and interpolation of new terms and groups of terms at any point in the schedule.

Notations are used in decimal fractions in a series 1, 2, 3, 4.......8, 9 and can be extended to 09, 1, 2, 21, 22, 23 ....3.......8, 91, 92, 93. The notations achieve the results by using significant symbols which are decimal fractions.

Notations are used as integers, not fractions. They rely upon leaving of blank number or gaps for its hospitability. This is called gap notation. Gaps are kept in the notation to accommodate new topics, e.g. a series 1, 2, 3, 5......,10, 11 can only be added as the gap left (at 4) and at the end of 10, 11. Ranganathan called them as gap notation and decimal fraction device. According to him gap device is not the only solution. A mathematical notation cannot be fully hospitable and gaps will remain there. The decimal fraction device will give a distinct helpful number to reach classes or isolates as it provides for the addition of digits.

Notation should be able to accommodate any number of coordinate subjects (extension of an existing array). The size of Arabic numbers can extend notations. Hence, only 1–8 are used. Digit 9 is used as empty digit and it is used ordinarily to individualise any class but as a repeater symbol introducing another sector of eight numbers, e.g. 1, 2, 3......8, 91, 92, 93 ....98.... The division of 9 in 91, 92 .....95, etc. will be used as sub-divisions of 9. Therefore, they are at para with digits 1–8, the digit 9 would never stand alone.

Decimal fractions have infinite hospitability but not fully. This could only be possible by fraction notation (decimal number or letters) designed to maintain the facet structure of the subject. Notation should easily be memorised, written, spoken in quoting, writing, typing and remembering, e.g. JGK and 610.

Structural qualities

(a) Notation is made up of digits.

(b) A digit is a single symbol in a notation.

(c) The total notation of digits in a notation is its base.

12.4 Structural Notation

(Structural vs. Non-structural = Hierarchy vs Non- hierarchy)

Classificatory structure: The structure of a subject is an arrangement of the concepts. Subjects at head are restricted in number.

We cannot drive out the traditional subjects as no such subjects are to be accommodated. It is necessary that relation is to be maintained/established to retain their system and value. General subjects are put before the specific subject. This is called Linear Method.

It requires two dimensional symbolism:

Example: Education

1	Primary education
11	Secondary education
12	University education
121	Graduate
122	Honours
123	Postgraduate
124	Research
2	Education for women

A set of term is called array-like.

Primary education

Secondary education

University education

Others are members of array. Sets of mutually exclusive terms are called facets.

All changes of characteristics will be called facets. In the above example there are two facets.

Classification structure has its chief elements hierarchy and facets are a statement about hierarchy. This hierarchy concept is found in integers or ordinal numbers.

Basic requirements of notations:

1. Ordinary relation between digits is known as conventional used sequence.
2. It should be easy to retain mentally. It needs no copying (Mnemonic concept).
3. It should retain brevity (shortness or conciseness) Brevity depends on the length of notational base, and uniformity in which digits are spaced out down with terms.
4. It should be easy to define (Easy notations).
5. It may be called simplicity of symbol.
6. Notation should be provinciable (De Grober).

   Although the notation is pure in the sense that one species of digits is used. The general requirement is that the symbols shall consist of consonants alternating with vowels.
7. It should be capable of unlimited growth. With the growth of knowledge 'new subjects' occur as fresh divisions which may be coordinates or subordinates or may be interpolated and extrapolated without the sequence already disturbing the existed sequence.

Structural Notation: A notation should exhibit not the order between the subjects, but also something of the structure of the classification scheme. The notation should be the symbolic inclusion or hierarchical relation between subjects by adding to the symbol for a given topic a further digit to represent one of the main divisions of the topic, a further digit to represent one of its part or components.

Example: 5   Science

55   Geological

551   Physical Geology

551.7   Strategraphy

551.79   Quaternary period

Advantage:

1. Symbols are readily remembered.
2. Search procedure for specific information normally proceeds hierarchically upward from the specific subject material to the successively more general containing subjects.

It offers similar facilities for mechanising the alphabetical subject index by chain procedure containing topic.

Notation can be devised to show the facet structure of the scheme together with the synthesis of topics belonging to different facets.

All modern schemes of classification attempt notational synthesis to some extent because the number of possible synthesis combination is so large that mnemonics supplementary tables are unavoidable if schedule length is to be kept within reasonable limits. This process is hardly carried out other than colon classification.

This difficulty may not arise in case of non-structural notation. Here, hierarchy may be broken by using the separation of symbols and leaving some digits as a gap for new subjects as shown below :

     b

     bm

     bp

     c

     b

Structural notations are lengthy and cannot accommodate new subjects which arise in the changing pattern of knowledge.

CC equates Zoology and Botany in hierarchical status,

while DC assigned one more symbol to Biology than to Botany, CC faced this situation and introduced Octave device. Symbol is taken as Octave to extend the array, like:

1

2

1

1

1

8

91

98

991

This device fulfils the requirement of extrapolation but fails to accommodate any concept in between the subjects. Octave device expresses the hierarchy. In DC '0' has also been used for expression like 0-9 but to set out 90 terms on two digits base 00-99, which accommodates 100 subjects. Ranganathan further used Greek letters.

Octave notation enables the notation to remain expressive digit. The use of Greek letters for interpolating new classes is not a permanent solution. No doubt that Ranganathan used 9 as octave notation but here 9 makes the digit lengthy and 9 lost his cementic status/value. It is more bad than the use of alphabetical base. This will be the coordinate base.

p	Here we can use as synthesizing
paf	digit for connecting in both
pab	components from other facets.
pal	The general effect is to emphasize
pp	the structural boundary between the last facet and those preceding it.
pc	Ranganathan uses indicator which does not allow interpolation in facet. Interpolation could then be achieved by adding a second numeral to a facet indicator behind which the new facet is to be inserted. This does not mean hierarchical relationship.

12.5 Non-Structural Notation

Here, interpolation is permitted. Non-structural notation is also unique in being able to conform to the canon of even distribution of base over terms. Here it is briefer than structural notation in all cases except when the number of terms in facets and array equals the number of digits in the base.

If we assume that one species is alone used, attenuated structural rotation will enable us to insert between two occupied consecutive digit p, q as follows:

p   sub-coordinate with q.

pa   compound of p and sub-division from other facet.

pb-p4   ad hoc divisions of p constitute the ultimate facet.

pzd   inserted coordinate of p and q.

q   sub-coordinate with p.

Interpolation between consecutive symbols as p and q would be achieved merely by adding a digit q and r.

With non-structured notation on further implication is possible, that is synthesising symbol together.

p   named instrument/marches

p   named instrument/suits

pz   named instrument

po   flute

pp   above

Hence, no system has been considered which has been completely non-structural with regard to facets. However, simple expressive hierarchical notation is relatively long because it virtually precludes even distribution of digits over terms and remains relatively long because it requires the use within the symbol of semantically empty digit, which is merely a signpost hierarchical status.

12.6 Sector Notation

12.6.1 Array in Notational Plane

The set of class numbers or isolate numbers is used to represent the classes or the ranked isolates, as the case may be, in an array and taken in the sequence of the classes or of the ranked isolates. This is maximum number of distinct class numbers or isolates numbers that can be accommodated in an array.

12.6.2 Empty Digit

A digit with ordinal value but without semantic value is known as empty digit. Usually the last digit of the species of digits is made an empty digit. In DC and UDC, the digit 9 is often used as an empty digit, except in very few cases. It can be used to derive any number of digits group to present coordinate idea.

In CC, the digits Z, 9 and z are used as empty digits, except in very few cases. The digit 0 (zero) is also used as empty digit, when it is not used as a connecting digit for phase and not used as a numeral in a chronological number (91). This multiple uses of digit '0' in arithmetic are shown below:

(a) Zero can be taken as both positive and negative.

(b) The result of multiplied; as a consequence.

(c) The quotient of dividing zero by zero may be taken as any number. In other words, it is indeterminate.

(d) Division of any number other than zero by zero is not permitted.

In CC, the digit "(" (started bracket) is also used as an empty digit. An empty digit becomes meaningful if it is added to some other digits.

12.6.3 Emptying Digit

It is for the purpose of interpolation between any two existing class numbers or isolate numbers in an array. Interpolation is necessary to adjust new ideas that crop up and require a position between any two already existing consecutive ideas.

Emptying digit deprives the cementic value of its preceding digit in a digit group and retains its ordinal value.

Example: In digit pair KX, X empties the sementic value of K, but retains its ordinal value.

K   — Zoology

KX — Animal husbandry
L — Medicine

The digit T, U, V, X, Y, Z are emptying digits.

12.6.4 Zone Formation

Each isolate in a normal array belongs to one and only one of the above four groups. Each of these groups is called a zone. It is convenient to arrange the isolates in an array in the sequence in their respective zones:

(a) Common isolate by enumeration.

(b) Special isolate by enumeration.

(c) Common isolate by non-enumeration.

(d) Special isolate by non-enumeration.

Advantage is taken to the digits belonging to different species of conventional symbols to six zones in an array consisting of the possible semantically rich digits. This is a convenience in discussion. The first digit of obvious species are 0, 9, 1 and A. We shall regard each of them as forming a single digit; that is, not counted a packet as a digit.

Further, we shall regard each of the following sets of digits as forming a species:

(9)	(00)
(a)	(z)
(1)	(8)
(A)	(Z)

The part of the array consisting of one species of digits shall be called a zone. Each zone may be denoted by a symbol using its first digit as shown in the following table:

Zone	Symbol	Digit in the array
1	(Z-0)	00 — 0
2	(Z-a)	ab — z
3	(Z-1)	1, 2 — 8
4	(Z-A)	AB — Z

5	(Z-(0))	(0) — (0)
	(Z-(a))	(a) — (z)
	(Z-(1))	(1) — (9)
	(Z-(A))	(A) — (Z)

5. Octave Notation: In 1876, Dewey, by a stroke of intuition, hit upon the idea of using the Indo-Arabic numerals 1 for the notational system of library classification. These are proved to be more simple than Roman capital letters. Accommodating classes and its sub-divisions in an important consideration. A fair decimal fraction notation came up as solution. DC managed to organise, in a fairly helpful sequence. The digit '9' was treated as a bundle of other residual classes which could not be accommodated in "1-8" divisions. The bundle of classes represented by '9' was then used for the next order array. The drawback of this "other device" was not apparent then. In term of notation, it meant mixing the coordinate classes with subordinate classes. As this did not affect adversely the arrangement of subjects, the device came to be used extensively in the different arrays.

CC: Ranganathan's fundamental idea helped to reshape and remodel the classification theory and practice. He realised the unhelpfulness of the "other device' which made the coordinate classes look like subordinate classes. This led to the other extreme of not using the digit '9' by itself to representing any isolate at all. He used '9' as a "doormat' which could allow the entity to pass through it making them into coordinates of the earliest set. The sacrificing of the ninth digit created the set of eight. The process of creation of sets of eight at the cost of the digit '9' was called Octave Device Notation. In Ranganathan's word "the other principles of D.C. has been extended in the what is called as 'Octave principle'. The digit '9' is not used to individualise any class."

6. Sector Notation: CC considers the following numbers in sequence:

Sector	one	1-8
Sector	two	91-98

Sector   Three   991-998
etc. etc.

The digit 9 is an emptying digit. Hence, all the above numbers are coordinate. They form a single array. These can be denoted by the symbols (S-1), (S-91), (S-991), etc. We can similarly have sectors in other zones also. Recognition of sectors in each array adds to the length of the array.

There is great potency in hospitality in array. The number of sectors used in a zone will depend on the number of emptying digits of zone brought into use. For convenience of use, the 8 number of sectors can be tabulated in each zone, with nos. one, two, etc. emptying digits.

(a) **Pure notation= Indo-Arabic Numerals**— The sequence 1-8, 91-98, 991-998, etc. though the number 91 has two digits can be considered. 9 has no value, similarly in sequence 991. '99' have no value. Though they have three digits, yet 91 is useful and meaningful as it is used to represent a class coordinate with the classes represented by the digits 1 to 8. This forms a single array in the digit 1-8, 91-98, 991-998, etc. The numbers 91-991 are treated as if each formed a single digit, the array 1 to 8 has been lengthened by sector device, with the help of emptying digit 9.

   (i)   The range 1 to 8 of the array is denoted by the symbol (S-1) and read as (S-1).

   (ii) The range 91-98 of the array is denoted by the symbol (S-91) and read as (S-91), each number is considered a sector notation.

   (iii) The range 991-998 of the array is denoted by the symbol (S-991) and read as (S-991) each number is considered as sector notation.

(b) **Roman Capital**—The array A-Y can be lengthened with the use of Z as emptying digit, into the array A....Z , ZA-ZY, ZZA-ZZY, etc. Where each one of the numbers ZA, etc. is treated as if it formed a single digit.

(c) **Roman Small**—Likewise the array a....y can be

lengthened with the use of z as empty digit in to the array a....y za........yy, zza......zzy etc.

(d) **Mixed base notation**—The mixed based may be considered as consisting of Roman smalls, Indo-Arabic numerals and Roman capitals. Let us make the digits z, 9, Z empty digits. We can use the digit '0' as an empty digit and with its ordinal value less than that of the digit '9'.

12.6.5 Notation System of some Schemes

DC

(1) One species of digit.

(2) It has a pure base.

(3) Notation is linear, right handed and decimal fractional.

(4) The dot used has neither momentic nor ordinal value It is dummy digit, Hence, it has been ignored in DC.

EC

(1) 26 Roman caps 10 Indo-Arabic numerals a dot.

(2) It has a mixed notation.

(3) Its notation is linear, right handed and decimal fractions.

(4) It does not use sector notation.

LC

(1) 10 Indo-Arabic numerals.

(2) 26 roman cap and one dot.

(3) It has a mixed base.

(4) Its .notation linear, right handed.

(5) But integral and non-decimal fractional.

(6) It does not use sector notation.

UDC

(1) 10 Indo-Arabic numerical.

(2) 26 common capitals, some punctuation marks, some Maths symbols.

(3) It has a mixed base.

(4) Its notations is linear, right handed and decimal fraction.

(5) It uses sector notation to some extent.

SC   (1)   10 Indo-Arabic numerals
            26 Roman capitals
            A dot.

      (2)   It has a mixed base.

      (3)   Its notation is linear & decimal fractional.

      (4)   It does not use sector notation.

B.C. (1)   9 Indo-Arabic numerals
            26 Roman capitals
            26 Roman small
            Some punctuation marks
            Some other unprovided digits.

      (2)   It has a mixed notation.

      (3)   Its notation is linear, right handed & decimal fractional.

      (4)   It does not use sector notation.

      (5)   Roman capitals are used.

      (6)   It has a pure base.

      (7)   It does not use decimal fractional.

With One Digit Chart

1	2	3 4	5 6		7	8	9	10 11	
Zone	Sector	Array Isolate Notation (AIN)	Total Array Isolate Number for		Leaving	Total Natural Number	Leaving for Emptying Digit	Total of Array Number for	
			Sector	Zone				Sector	Zone
1	(s-a)	a,b .....z	23	23	1 & 0	26	z	22	22
2	(s-1)	1,2.........9	9	9	1,$\bar{0}$	9	9	8	8
3	(S-A)	A,B.....Z	24	24	(i)(1)(0)	26	Z	23	23
4	S(a)	(a),(b)....z	23	23		26	(z)	(22)	(22)
5	S(1)	(1),(2),...(.9)	9	9		9	(9)	(8)	(8)
6	S(A)	(A),(b).....(Z)	24	24	(I) ($\bar{0}$)	26	(Z)	(23)	(23)
			112	112	10	122	6	106	106

(G1)

	Leaving for Quasi Isolate	Total array no. for sector	Counting brackets as a digit
1	a	21	
2	1	7	
3	A	22	
4	9	21	21
5	1	7	7
6	A	22	22
	6	100	50

With Two Digit Chart
Emptying digit
z 9Z = 3

(1) With three digits leaving for Q1   **(3)**

					1-8	-8	1	7
00a	00y	-22	00	21	90-a-90y	-22	a	21
001	008	-8	1	7	901-908	-8	1	7
00A	00y	-23	A	22	90A-90y	-23	A	22
0a	0y	-22	a	21	9a-9y	-22	a	21
0za	0zy	-22	a	21	9za-9zy	-22	9	21
0z1	0z8	-8	1	7	9z1-9z8	-8	1	7
0zA	0zy	-23	A	22	9zA-9zy	23	A	22
01	08	-8	1	7	91-98	8	1	7
09a	09y	-22	a	21	99a-99y	22	a	21
091	098	-8	1	8	991-998	8	1	7
09A	09y	-23	A	22	99A-99Y	23	A	22
0A	0y	-23	A	22	9A-9Y	23	A	22
0Za	0Zy	-22	a	21	9Za-9Zy	22	a	21
0Z1	0Z8	-8	1	7	9Z1-9Z8	8	1	7
0ZA	0ZY	23	A	22	9ZA-9ZY	23	a	22

265	15	250

273	16	257

(Q1) – QUASI 'ISOLATE'

(2)		(Q1)										
a	-	y	-	22	a	21	A	-	Y	-23	A	22
zoa	-	zoy	-	22	a	21	Zoa	-	Zoy	-22	a	21
zo1	-	zo8	-	8	1	7	Zo1	-	Z08	-8	1	7
zoA	-	zoy	-	23	A	22	ZoA	-	Z0Y	-23	A	22
za	-	zy	-	22	a	21	Za	-	Zy	-22	a	21
zza	-	zzy	-	22	a	21	Zza	-	Zzy	-22	a	21
zz1	-	zz8	-	8	1	7	zz1	-	Zz8	-8	1	7
zzA	-	zzy	-	23	A	22	ZzA	-	ZzY	-23	A	22
z1	-	z8	-	8	1	7	Z1	-	Z8	-8	1	7
z9a	-	z9y	-	22	9	21	Z9a	-	Z9y	-.22	a	21
z91	-	z98	-	8	1	7	Z91	-	Z98	-8	1	7
z9A	-	z9y	-	23	A	22	Z9A	-	Z9y	-23	A	22
zA	-	zy	-	23	A	22	ZA	-	ZY	-23	A	22
zZa	-	zZy	-	22	a	21	ZZa	-	ZZy	-22	a	21
zZ1	-	zZ8	-	8	1	7	ZZ1	-	ZZ8	-8	1	7
zZA	-	zZy	-	23	A	22	ZZA	-	ZZY	-23	A	22

	287	16	271		288	16	272

Total = 1113

12.6.6 Group Notation

A Decimal fraction notational system in which each number consists of two and only two rich digits; or three and only three rich digits; as so on; and does not include an empty digit. The numbers of a group system are deemed to form a single array.

Indo-Arabic numbers:

Two digit group system Three digit group system	Indo-Arabic Numerals	Roman caps	Indo-Arabic & Roman caps
	64	529	961
	512	12167	29791
111...118 11A...11Y	=11-18 21-28	AAA-AAY,ABA	A1-18
121...123 12A..12Y	= 81-88=64	AYA-AYY,BAA-	AA-AY
181-188, 18A-18Y1, A1-	=111-118,121-128	BAY	B1-B8
1A8 1AA-1AY	=181-188,211-218	BBA-BBY,BYA-	BA-BY
1B1-1B8, 1BA-1BY, 1Y1-	221-228, 281-288	BYY	YA-Y8
1y8,1YA-1YY	811-218,821-828	YAA-BAY,BBB-	YA-YY
	831-888=512	BBY	=961
= 211-218		BYA-BYY=12167	
and as such with			
811-818,81A-81Y,821-			
828,82A-82Y			
8B1-8B8,8BA-8BY,8YA-			
8Y8,8YA-8YY			
A11-A18			
B11-B18,B1A-B1Y			
Y11-Y18,Y1A-Y1Y			
= 29791			

Decision:

1. Use Sector System—if the number of number to be accommodated in the array is less than 24.

2. Use Group System—if the number of numbers to be accommodated in the array is more than 24.

3. Use either System—if the number of numbers to be accommodated in the array is 24.

1. Zone (Z-0) Written simply as (Z-0), consists of all numbers in the array beginning with the digit 0.

2. Zone (z-a) written simply as (z-a) consists of all the numbers in an array beginning with Roman small.

3. Zone (Z-1) written simply as (Z-1) consists of all the numbers in an array beginning with the Indo-Arabic numerals.

4. Zone (Z-A), written simply (Z-A) consists of all the numbers in an array beginning with the Roman capital numerals.

5. Z (Z-(>), written simply (Z-(,), consists of all the pocket numbers in the array.

13

Book Number

In CC, book number is known as canon of Book Number.

Ranganathan: "A scheme of book numbers should be provided with a scheme of book numbers to individualise the documents having the same class of knowledge as their ultimate class."

There are many methods to individualise the documents under the same specific subject. The following are some standard practices:

1. Writing first three alphabets of the author's surname.
2. Translation of the author's name into an ordinal number.
3. Translation of the year of publication of documents.
4. Translation by the colon book number system.

CC: The book number of a book is a symbol used to fix its position relatively to the other books having the same ultimate class.

The book number of a book is the translation of the names of certain of its specified features into the artificial language of ordinal numbers.

The book number consists of an intelligible series of things linked together (concatenation) of one or more of the following symbols:

1. 24 Roman capitals got by omitting I and O.

2. 23 Roman small got by omitting i, l, o.

3. The punctuation mark—dot, hyphen, semicolon and colon (. - ; :).

4. 10 Indo-Arabic numerals.

5. The digits are written from left to right.

Ranganathan has designed the book numbers by introducing facet analysis. It takes into consideration all the possible characteristics of physical embodiment to form the book number as language, form of exposition, year of publication, number of volumes, author of the book, etc.

[L] [F] [Y] [A], [V] — [S] ; [c] : [Cr]

L: Language in which the document is written (Language number)

F : Form of document.

Y : Year of publication of the document (Year number).

A : Accession number part of the document.

V : Volume number of the document.

S : Supplement number of the document.

C : Copy number of the document.

Cr : Criticism number of the document.

L = (a) Use of [L] facet will be required if the books are in languages other than the favoured language of a library.

(b) Many libraries prefer to have altogether a different sequence under different languages, where language number will be a part of the sequence number.

F = Use of [F] facet will also be rare.

Y = [Y] facet is the major domo (The facet with the responsibility of general management) here. It will find place under each book.

A = [A] facet will come if more than two works on a subject have appeared in a year.

V-S = [V]-[S] will appear if the document is in many volumes or is appearing in supplements, respectively.

C = [C] facet will be required because the number of copies of a book is often more than one.

Cr = [Cr] facet will be required to indicate that one work is in criticism or attached to another work on the same subject.

Special features

1. Book numbers will individualise each document in a library.

2. No two documents will have the same number.

3. Perfect individualisation is possible.

13.1 [L] – Language Number

The language number is got by translating the name of the language in which the book is written into appropriate symbols in accordance with the language.

The favoured language of a library is the language in which the majority of the books of the library are found written.

In the case of a book consisting of two or more commentaries of a classic but not containing the classic itself, the most popular of the languages in which a commentary occurs should be used to construct the language number.

In the case of a book belonging to a main class other than 'Literature' if it is in the favoured language or if the language to be used to construct the language number is the favoured one, the language number need not be written.

In the case of a book belonging to the main class 'literature' if the language of the book is the same as the language of the literature, the language number need not be written.

For example if library's favoured language is English, *Pustakalaya, Suchikaran; Ek Adhyayan* by R.L. Tiwari written in Hindi published in 1971 will get book number as = 152 N71.

In the case of a periodical publications, the language number need not be written.

13.2 Form Number

The form number is got by translation the name of the form of exposition into appropriate symbols in accordance with the form schedule.

It may be stated that the form number need not be written if the book is in the conventional form. Thus, the majority of books in a library will not need the form facet in their book number.

Form number beginning with 'w' is not applicable to a book in the main class 'Literature'.

13.3 Year Number

The year number is got by translating the number of the year of publication into appropriate symbols in accordance with the time schedule.

If preferred, libraries, whose books are mostly recent ones, may use the following special chronological schedule for the Book Number :

A	before 1880	K	1960 to 1969	U	2050 to 2059
B	1880 to 1889	L	1970 to 1979	V	2060 to 2069
C	1890 to 1899	M	1980 to 1989	W	2070 to 2079
D	1900 to 1909	N	1990 to 1999	X	2080 to 2089
E	1910 to 1919	P	2000 to 2009	Y	2090 to 2099
F	1920 to 1929	Q	2010 to 2019	ZA	2100 to 2109
G	1930 to 1939	R	2020 to 2029	ZB	2110 to 2119
H	1940 to 1949	S	2030 to 2039	ZC	2120 to 2129
J	1950 to 1959	T	2040 to 2049	ZD	2130 to 2139, etc.

In case of periodical publication the year, covered by the volume, should be used for the year number.

If the volume of a period publication covers two or more years, the earliest of them should be used.

If the issues of a periodical publication, covering a year, form two or more volumes or parts, such volumes or parts should be regarded as an indivisible set and the rules of accession number should be applied.

All the books will require year number.

Viz = elements of classification published in 1962

Book no. = N62 or K2

A = A stands for accession part of the book number. In case there are two or more books having the same class number and the book number based on above rules, these will be individualised by sequence of accession.

Example: Test books of Physics/Introduction of Physics and Elements of Physics written in English language and published in 1972.

1. Class number 'C' in CC.
2. Up to year of publication will be same for all three books- N72 or L2.

But these will be individualised by accession number.

1. Textbook of Physics   N72 or L2 only
2. Introduction to Physics   N721 or L21
3. Elements of Physics   N 722 or L22

In the accession part of the book, number consists of more than one digit, it should be read as an integer and not as a decimal fraction.

V stand for volume number. It will be required only in case of multi-volumed books. Volumes of the set are to be individualised by putting a dot after the year number or accession part of the book number, as the case may be and adding the number of volume in Indo-Arabic numerals.

Example: Vol. I of the set published in 1962 = N62.1

Vol. II of the set published in 1962 = N62.2

A multi-volume book hold the following conditions:

1. The set possesses a common index.
2. The same sequence of pages is continued throughout all the volumes of the set.
3. The subject matter is so distributed among the volumes of the set that it is not helpful to treat each volume as a separate book.

If the volume number consists of more than one digit, it should be read as an integer and not as a decimal fraction.

The year of publication of an indivisible set is the year in which the earliest published volume of the set is published.

S stands for supplement number. A volume having supplementary volume will have book number of the corresponding main volume followed by a 'dash' and supplement number in Indo-Arabic numerals.

Example: Book published in 1969   =   N69
First supplement   =   N69—1
Second supplement   =   N69—2

If a supplementary volume relates to more than one volume of an indivisible set of volume, the number of supplement should be attached to the book number of the last of such volumes in the set.

The digit or digits thus added after the 'dash' may be called the 'supplement number'. If supplement number consists of more than one digit, it should be read as an integer and not as a decimal fraction.

C stands for copy number. If a library is having more than one copy of the book, the copy number will be required from second copy onwards. Copy number is attached by the connecting symbol 'semi colon' :

Example= First copy of the book   =   N72
          Second copy of the same book   =   N72;   1
          Third copy of the same book   =   N72;   2
          Fourth copy   =   N72;   3
          Hundredth copy   =   N72;   99
          Hundred & first copy   =   N72;   100
          nth copy   =   N72;   n-1

If a copy number is in more than one digit, it should be read as an integer and not as decimal fraction. Successive, non-successive editions of an ordinary book, without any substantial or distinctive changes, should be treated as copies of the book.

Cr stands for criticism number. If a book is not a classic, and another book is written on it say criticism, the best use of the second book will be only if it is lying on the shelf near the host book.

The book number for second book will be that of the host book followed by ':g'. The connecting symbol for criticism number is colon.

If the criticism of a book comes in more than one, these are to be numbered as 1, 2, 3, etc.

Example

(1) Colon classification published in 1969   =   qN60

(2) Criticism of colon classification   =   qN60:g
     published in 1972

(3) Criticism of colon classification   =   qN60:g1
     published in 1974

13.4 Accession Part of the Criticism Number

The book number of the second, third, etc. associated book of the same host book should consist of that of the first followed by the digit 1, 2 etc. respectively.

The number so added after the criticism number may be called the accession part of the criticism number.

If the accession part of the criticism number consists of two or more digits, it should be read as an integer and not as a decimal fraction.

13.5 Collection Number

This canon demands that various sequences that are maintained in a library should be duly specified. The sequences are necessary in a library for prompt services. Each sequence should be given different symbols.

Example:

Name of Sequence	Collection No.	CC	DC
Undersize documents	Underline book No.	[X [JX	330 J5
Oversize documents	Overline book No.	X J5	330 J5
Worn out books	Underline and Overline book No.	X J5	330 J5
Rare book	RB	RB X J5	RB 330 J5
Reading Room	RR	RR X J5	RR 330 J5
Textbook	TC	TC X J5	TC 330 J5
Political Science Department	WD	WD X J5	WD 330 J5

Collection	Collection Number
Reading Room	RR
Secondary	SC
Tertiary	TC
Periodicals	PC
Physics Department	CD
Law Department	ZD

Example:

Class No.	330
Book No.	J5
Collection No.	RR

With Two Digits

1	2	3	4	5	6	7	8	9	10
1	(s-a)	a,b-y	22		i,?,o,z	A	21		
	(s-za)	za-zy	22				21		
	(s-z1)	z1-z8	8	75			7		
	(s-zA)	zA-zy	23		9	1	22	71	
2	(s-1)	1,2-8	8				7		
	(s-q9)	99-9y	22				21		
	(s-91)	91-98	8	61			7		
	(s-9A)	9A-9y	23		I,O,Z,A	A	22	57	
3	(s-A)	A-y	23				22		
	(z-za)	za-zy	22				21		
	(s-z1)	z1-z8	8	76			7		
	(s-ZA)	ZA-Zy	23		i,?,o,z		22	72	
4	(s-(a)	(a)-(y)	22			a	21		
	(s-(za)	(za)-(zy)	22				21		
	(s-z1)	(z1)-(z8)	8	75			7		71
	(s-zA)	(zA)-(zy)	23		9	1	22	71	
5	(s)-(1)	(1)-(8)	8				7		
	(s)-(91)	(9a)-9y)	22				21		
	(s)-(91)	(91)-(98)	8	61			7		57
	(s)-(92)	(9A)-(9y)	23		I,O,Z,A	A	22	57	
6	(s-(A)	(A)-(y)	23				22		
	(s-(za)	(za)-(zy)	22				21		
	(s-(Z)	(z1)-(z8)	8	76			7		72
	(s-(ZA)	(zA)-(zy)	23		I,O,Z,A	A	22	72	
			424	424	16	6		400	200

Emptying Digit (Combination):

zz	9z	Zz
z9	99	Z9
zZ	9Z	ZZ
3	3	3	= 9

14

Postulation Approach

Definition: The purpose of the postulation approach to classification is to help a scheme in visualising the discipline of classification objectively. It also checks the scheme against any confused thinking. This is done by stating certain postulates (Fundamental principles of universal validity in a field) as a starting point.

The Nero Standard Dictionary defines the term postulate in the following words:

Only three meanings are given here:

(i) A proposition, claim or basis or argument laid down as well known; too plane to require proof; a self-evident truth.

(ii) A self-evident statement regarding the possibility of a thing.

(iii) A condition preceding must be in use to explain or a account for a thing; a piece is postulate of prosperity.

Postulates are assumptions used as the basis for the development of any system of thought or the framing and the working of any system of techniques. Dr. Ranganathan observed, a postulate is a statement about which we cannot use either of the 'epithets', 'right' or 'wrong'. We can speak postulates as 'helpful' or 'unhelpful'. Here, postulates are helping in classifying a document.

There are certain facets and experiences, based on the assumptive principles, in the field of knowledge and their exposition. Postulates are derived by adopting both the process one after the other in a series, resulting into the spiral of scientific method.

There is multidimensional expansion of knowledge eventually reminding us the universal form of Lord Krishna revealed to Arjun. It was possible for him on account of his having been endowed for the moment with transcendental regarded as the best universal classification of our time the postulational approach approximates to transcendental approach and with its help, any subject in the universe of knowledge be visualised, analysed and synthesized. This is the gift of Dr. Ranganathan to library profession.

Postulation approach gathers together the genius components of the subjects of a document and arranges them into the homogeneous sequences of symbols or ordinal value—the class number. The postulates are really concerned with the analysis of any subject into its kernel ideas and their arrangement and synthesis subject approach is a common approach of readers. The aim of classifying is the gradual progression from general to specific subject. It is for the reason that the process of classification starts from the idea plane. It then goes through the verbal plane for language is the medium of communication of thoughts or ideas. It finally arrives at the notational plane of class number.

Postulate secure a more or less helpful sequence among the known class of knowledge. Postulates are of use in finding a more or less helpful place for newly emerging class among the already existing ones with little disturbance of their own established sequence.

In colon classification, sequence of canonical classes is also determined in a more or less helpful way. The new basic classes are assigned to one or the other main classes and the canonical classes. They are also arranged in helpful way according to some definite principles.

In classificatory terminology, we may say that the process of classification is carried out on three planes, i.e. Idea, Verbal and Notational plane and there are postulates to regulate the work of classification in each of these three planes.

The postulates for Idea and Verbal planes are similar to practically all the classification schemes of today. But the postulates for Notational plane differ from scheme to scheme. Here are the postulates for these three planes as isolated by Ranganathan.

14.1 Idea Plane

1. Postulates of Fundamental Categories: Every subject is composed of a basic class. It may include isolates which are manifestations of one or more five fundamental categories (PMSET) or an Antiriorising Common Isolate.

2. Postulates of Basic Facet: Basic class and Antiriorising common isolates are those enumerated as such by a scheme of classification.

3. Postulation of Isolate Facet: Personality or P, Matter or M, Energy or E, Space or S and Time or T are five and only Five fundamental categories. The five fundamental categories fall in the sequence of PMEST, if arranged in the decreasing sequence of their concreteness.

4. Postulate of Rounds for Energy: Energy may manifest itself in one and the same subject more than once, that is, in more than one round.

5. Postulate of Rounds for Personality and Matter: It is possible for the manifestation of personality and matter to occur after (1E), again after (2E), again after (3E) and so on; that is, any round.

6. Space S and Time T occur in the end of a subject as space que space and time que time.

7. Postulate of Level: Save the fundamental category E each of the other fundamental categories may manifest itself more than once in two or more levels. So is the case of matter, space and time.

8. Postulate of Concreteness: The five fundamental categories fall into the following sequence when arranged according to their decreasing concreteness: P,M,E,S,T.

9. Postulate of Sequence: The basic facet of subject should be put first; and the other facet should be arranged thereafter in the sequence of the decreasing concreteness of the fundamental categories of which they are respectively taken to be manifestation, provided there is not more than one basis facet and not more than one manifestation of any fundamental category.

Each postulate has a practical implication on the nature of knowledge and the modes of their formation in documents. Analysis of the specific subject becomes simpler through these postulates.

14.2 Verbal Plane

The verbal plane is concerned with the terminology of a scheme of classification. Terms of vital importance in the transition of an idea to its notation set out as much in a scheme of classification. Postulates for verbal plane have not yet worked out.

14.3 Notational Plane

One essential feature of postulates for notational plane is their variations with the particular scheme of classification in use. They are implied in Colon Classification, the Universal Decimal Classification and to some extent in the Bibliographic Classification.

Postulate of connecting symbols: The connecting symbols to be inserted in front of various kinds of facets are given below:

Facet	Connecting symbols
(P)	,
(M)	;
(E)	:
(S)	.
(T)	'

(a) **Postulate for Omission of Connecting Symbols, Form 1**—CC the connecting symbol need not be inserted before (P), if it immediately follows (BC). L45 (L Basic Class Medicine, 45 (P) Lungs).

(b) **Postulate for Omission of Connecting Symbols, Form 2**—The connecting symbol need not be inserted before (2P), (3P), etc. If these follow immediately after (E), (2E), etc. L45:421:6253. 44'N.

The omission of connecting symbol which in this case is a comma between 4(E) and 21(P), similarly between 6(E) and 253 (3P) is due to the postulate stated above.

In every scheme of classification, the notation comprises of digit of various species. So also in the colon classification. The special feature of CC symbols is that each digit of each species is consciously given an ordinal value in respect to one another. This fixes their relative position and ultimately results in the helpful sequence. CC has following connecting symbols.

There are four 'Dots' or postulates to impart accuracy :

(a) Don't bring a comma before the second round first level personality immediately following the E.

(b) Don't bring a comma before the first round first level personality following the BC.

(c) Don't bring a comma before the third round first level of personality immediately following 'E'.

(d) Don't bring any connecting symbol before AC1.

In other words, some of the postulates are given below:

(a) Class number may consist of one or different types of symbols or digits.

(b) Digits may be either substantive digits (significant digits) or connecting digits.

(c) There may be a different zones of digits allotted to respective Zones of the idea plane.

(d) There may be sectorising digit under each type of substantive digits.

(e) Certain connecting digits may be required in notation to indicate the frozen idea in a specific subject.

(f) Each digit will have its ordinal value or place value in the sequence of arrangement.

(g) Decimal numbers suit well the needs of notation.

14.4 Principles of Deciding Sequence

There are some principles which are of immense use in deciding the sequence of facets. Others may crop up.

1. Commodity-Raw-Material-Transformation Principles: In the spinning of cotton into yarn, yarn comes first: cotton comes second and spinning comes last.

Yarn	Cotton	Spinning
(First)	(Second)	(Last)
(Commodity)	(Raw material)	(Transformed part)

2. Cow-Calf Principle: This principle points out that when a cow is purchased no extra price is paid for the calf, the cow automatically accompanies the calf. This principle determines the sequence of facets to be brought together in the same round in a classification.

3. Whole-Organ Principle: If there are two facets and one exhibits an entity as a whole and the other one of its organs, the sequence is best obtained by bringing the former first.

Entity as a whole-organ

4. Act and Action–Actor Principle: When any four facets fall in mutual relation their sequence would be governed by this principle.

5. Wall–Picture Principle: This principle arranges the facets where earlier one is to introduce the later, the former is to precede in such a case.

14.5 Steps

To organise the classification process so mechanically and so perfectly that faulty results are obtained, we cannot dispense with these postulates and principles. The process of classification is divided in various steps — 0-8.

Example:

STEP-0 (Raw Title): Flood relief for rural folk in Assam up to 1950.

Note: In this step, the raw title of a document is written.

STEP-1 (Expressive Title): Treatment by "relief in Assam up to 1950 for rural folk" subjected to social pathology caused by "Flood in Sociology".

Note: This step belongs to the verbal plane, it is derived from the title. In this step all ellipses are filled up. The name of the basic class is supplied if it is not already explicitly mentioned.

STEP-2 (Kernel Title): Treatment relief Assam 1950 Rural Folk social pathology Flood Sociology.

Note: This step belongs to verbal plane. It is derived from the expression title. In this step all the auxiliary words are dropped and only terms expressing the relevant facets of the subject are retained.

STEP-3 (Analysed Title): Treatment [2E] relief [2P] Assam (S) 1950 (T).

Rural folk (P) Sociology(E) Flood [2P] Sociology [BC].

Note: This step belongs to the idea plane. It is derived from the kernel title. In the step each kernel terms is marked by the type of facet it represents manifestation of fundamental categories is shown (BC) or (ACI) is also analysed.

1. Here, sociology is the basic class of the subject.

2. Two energy isolates "Social pathology" and "Treatment" present a problem in arrangement. The wall picture principle gives the arrangement "Social pathology" and "Treatment". The later is possible only if the former is conceded.

3. Of the three personality isolates— Relief, Rural folk and Flood, each must be assigned to its respective round. Round end with E and according to the seventh postulate of the idea plane, consider social pathology which is the first round energy. This is action. The act and the entity acted upon is Rural folk. The actor of the entity acting is food. Applying the act and action-act or principle Rural Folk has to be put before social pathology —that is the first round and food has to be put after social pathology—that is, in the second round.

4. Then consider treatment, which is the second round energy. This is Action. Flood is the entity acted upon. Relief is the Actor. Therefore, by the act- and action-Actor principle, Rural folk has to be put before treatment, that is, in the second round. And relief has to be put after treatment — that is, in the third round.

5. Assam is the only time isolate. It should come in the last round by postulate 193.

6. 1950 is the only time isolate. It should come in the last round isolate by postulate 193.

7. This is facet analysis.

STEP-4 (Transformed Title): Sociology (BC) Rural Folk (P) Social Pathology (E) Flood [2P] Treatment (2E) Relief (3P) Assam 1950 (T).

Note: This step belongs to the verbal plane. It is derived from the analysed title. It is guided by the symbols attached to the terms already on the basis of these principles and postulates. The kernel terms sociology has been brought first in accordance with postulates 192 from the idea plane. Other kernel terms are arranged according to the postulate 193.

STEP-5 (Title in Standard Terms): Sociology (BC) rural Folk (P) Social Pathology (E) Flood (2P) Treatment (2E) Relief work (3P) Assam (S) 1950 (T).

Note: This step belongs to verbal plane. The arrangement is just the same, but every kernel term is replaced by the standard term as found in the scheme of classification used. Relief is the only kernel term replaced by its equivalent found in the concerned schedule of CC.

STEP-6 (Title in Facet Number): Y (BC) 31 [P] 43[E]55 (2P) 6(2E) 7(3P) 4477 (S) N5(T) (Y31.4355 :67.4477 'N5)

Note: This step belongs to notational plane. In step 6, the standard terms are translated into facet formula from the respective schedules. This step is important for it moves the work from the verbal plane to the notational plane.

STEP-7 (Synthesized Class Number): Y31:4355:67.4477 'N5.

Note: This step belongs to notational plane. In this step facet symbols are removed and the connecting symbols are inserted according to the postulates for Notational plane. This is called facet synthesis.

STEP-8 (Verification): This step involves the reverse translation from the ordinal language to the natural language, that is from the notational plane to the verbal plane.

By verification we can check the CC extensiveness of class number. The links which are sought in the chain can be used to construct class index entries by chain procedure.

By this example, the followed step, we can infer some of the helpful features of the postulation approach. These are :

1. Postulation approach removes too much dependence on the flair of the classifier.

2. The process, being mechanical and scientific, lessens the strain of the classifier.

3. This admits of one and only one co-extensive class number.

4. This gives a definite systematic subject approach. Therefore, a classifier can be sure of his class number. This is not so in the other scheme.

5. This helps in detecting any wrong step taken in the process of classifying micro thought. This is not possible in the other schemes.

6. Being a scientific method, it is of great help in documentation which has its emphasis on nascent micro-thought.

7. Step by step process is smooth and rhythmic.

8. It is versatile process as it admits of dealing with any subject however complicated.

9. It serves the twofold purpose of classification as well as indexing.

14.6 Postulation Approach: An Analysis

Postulation approach established itself as a scientific method with a multifocal utility. Its application to every possible document brings macro or micro proliferation. It has mechanical and scientific characteristics which have introduced an effective smoothness in its working.

A Study in the Ability of Genius for Higher Science Education

Step 0 = Raw Title—A study in the ability of genius for higher science education.

Step 1 = Full Title—A study in the ability of genius (Psychology) for higher science education.

Step 2 = Kernel Title—Ability genius psychology (Biasing) higher science education (of, for and in omitted).

Step 3 = S Analysed Title—Ability [E] Genius [P] Psychology [BC] (Biasing) Higher [P] Science [SD1] Education [BC].

Ability is problem [E].

Genius is group, hence [p].

Psychology [BC] of genius [P].

Science qualifies the grade higher [P] in education [BC].

= There are two [BC]—Psychology and Education, hence subject device.

Here science is not main class.

Step 4 = Transformed Title—

1st Phase = Psychology [BC] Genius [P] Ability [E] [Biasing].

2nd Phase = Education (BC) Higher [P] Science [SD1].

Step 5 = Title in Standard Terms—

(1) All terms except higher are standard terms (CC).

(2) The term 'higher' has been replaced by term 'University'.

(3) In DC the term higher is a standard term.

Phase I — Psychology [BC] Genius [P] Ability [E].

Phase II — Education [BC] University [P] Science [SDI].

Step 6 = Title in Numbers—

  CC = S[BC] 61 [P] 73 [E] b(Biasing) T(BC) 4 [P] A[SD1].

  DC = 15 [BC] 1 [P] 1 [E] 37 [BC] 8 [P] 5 [SD1].

In DC, we find that 1 [E] comes before 1 [P] in notation.

Step 7 = Synthesised Number—

CC— S61:73.ob T4(A)

In CC = S connects 73.ob connect the second phase and ( ) connects A (SD1).

DC— 151.1 or 378 or 507.11

Step 8 = Verification by Reverse Translation—

CC. S Basic class
61 Personality
73 Energy facet
b (biasing) Inter-subject relation
T Basic class
4 Personality

Example: Simple specific subject

Step 0   = Raw title—Principles of Biology
Step 1   = Full title
Step 2   = Kernel title—Principles Biology
Step 3   = Analysed title—Principle Biology (BC)
Step 4   = Transformed title—Term brought after Biology
Step 5   = Standard term—Biology
Step 6   = CC   G
(analysed) DC   574
Step 7   = Synthesised Number
            71   CC   G
            72   DC   574
Step 8   = Verification by Reverse Translation
            In CC G—Biology   ⌐ No other facet
            In DC 574—Biology   ⌐ is in value

Examples: Feeding of cattles in India

Step 0 = Raw title = Feeding of cattles in India.

Step 1 = Full title = Feeding of cattles in India in "Animal Husbandry".

Step 2 = Kernel title = Feeding, cattle, India, Animal Husbandry.

Step 3 = Analysed title = Feeding [E] Cattle [P] India [S] Animal Husbandry [BC].

Step 4 = Transformed title = Animal Husbandry [BC] Cattle [P] [Feeding][E].

Step 5 = Titles in standard terms = Animal Husbandry [BC] Cattle [P] Feeding [E] India [S]

Step 6 = Titles in numbers [Notational plane]

CC KZ [BC] 2 [P] 1 [E] 44 [s]

DC 656 [BC] 2 [P] 084 [E] 954 [S]

Step 7 = Synthesised number

CC— KZ2 :1.44

DC— 636.20840954

In CC— To connect 1 of [E] and is used to connect 44 [S].

In DC— To connect 2 [2] and 0 is used to connect 954 of [S].

Step 8 = KZ is basic class

2 is personality facet

1 is energy facet

44 is space facet.

Meaning thereby – "Feeding of Cattles in India".

In DC = 636 is basic class

2 is personality facet

084 is energy facet

954 is space facet.

Meaning thereby— "Feeding of Cattles in India".

A common personality or matter isolate may start a round.

Verbal Plane— 2 Postulates:

1. Each specific subject must belong to a basic class, whose term should be added to the title of the document.

2. Terms used in specific subject may be compound nature which should be broken into the constituent kernel term.

(These help in the treatment of specific subjects).

Notational Plane—7 Postulates

1. Class number may consist of one or different types of symbols or digits.
2. Digits may be either substantive digits or connecting digit.
3. There may be a sectorising digit under each type of substantive digit.
4. There may be different zones in digits allotted to it respective zones of the idea plane.
5. Certain connecting digits may be required in notation to indicate the frozen ideas in the specific subjects.
6. Each digit will bare its ordinal value or place value in the sequence of arrangement.
7. Decimal numbers suit well the needs of notation.

Stages of the application of postulates:

Step 0 — Raw title—Show title as it appears on the document deals with the work in idea plane.

Step 1 — In this step we add the name of the main class if it is not included in title.

Step 2 — We show only those terms which denote kernel ideas, this means auxiliary words like of, in, for, etc.

Step 3 — Kernel ideas represented by their respective terms are analysed. They are branded according to postulates.

Step 4 — These terms are arranged in a sequence about which postulates exist.

Step 5 — The non-standard terms are replaced by the term adopted in the scheme.

Step 6 — Each term is translated into numbers.

Step 7 — The various numbers are connected with each other by the symbols prescribed by the postulates.

Step 8 — Examines the entire process in the light of postulates.

Postulation Approach

Standard Dictionary

(i) A proposition, claim and basis or arrangement laid down as well as known, to plane to require proof; a self-evident truth.

(ii) A self-evident statement regarding the possibility of a thing.

(iii) A condition preceded that must be in use to explain or an account for a thing; as peace is a postulate of prosperity.

Ranganathan says that in this method of approach one is not bound by any preconceived meta physical or other ideas and not even by factual experiences. Certain postulates are assumed and all the implications are marked out.

Postulation approach means:

1. There are certain facts and experiences, based on assumed principles in the field of knowledge and their expositions.

2. These principles are supported by the facets and this becomes too simple to be doubled.

3. Whether postulates are derived by both the adopted processes.

Types of postulates:

1. Postulates for the idea plane.

2. Postulates for the verbal plane.

3. Postulates for the notational plane.

Idea plane — Some of the important postulates of idea plane are:

(a) There are five fundamental categories under different main classes. More than one main class may form a specific subject.

(b) Every characteristic can be assigned to one and only one fundamental category.

(c) Division of universe on the basis of characteristics may yield classes containing only wholes, portions, organs and constitutes, respectively.

(d) The first manifestation of energy in a basic class in its first round energy facet, second in second round and so on.

(e) An energy facet can have only one array.

(f) The first round is started by the basic class.

(g) In any round many numbers or levels of personality and matter can occur consecutively.

(h) There is no level for array.

15

Focus and Facet

The facets of a class are determined with the help of certain characteristics, which are applied to the subject for its divisions. A certain number of train of characteristics will yield an equal number of facets of a class. The totality of isolates formed on the basis of the first train of characteristics is a first level facet. Similarly, the totality of the isolates formed on the basis of the second train of characteristics is the second level facet.

Palmer and Wells: "The whole group of divisions or foci produced when a subject is divided according to a train of characteristics."

Ranganathan: "The totality of the divisions of a basic class based on single train of characteristics is said to constitute one of its facets."

J.S. Mill: "The total sub-classes resulting from the application of a single characteristic is called a facet."

15.1 Focus

An individual member, sub-class or isolate within a facet is called focus. According to Palmer and Wells: "Any specific division of a subject area to one characteristic, i.e. any single division of a facet." Ranganathan described it as "each division in a facet is said to be an Isolate Focus or simply an isolate." It means:

(a) Single characteristics as a part of one class.

(b) Sub-class, individual member or an isolate.

Example: (i)

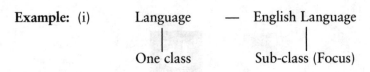

(ii)

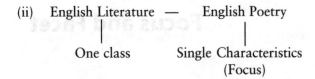

(iii) Compound Subject

"Treatment of tuberculosis of the lungs by X-rays."

Medicine (Lungs): Tuberculosis: X-ray treatment

Lungs— Personality characteristics

Tuberculosis— Problem characteristics

X-rays treatment— Handling characteristics.

Hence, these are:

(a) Organ facet.

(b) Problem facet.

(c) Handling facet.

'Medicine' is the focus in the basic facet of the subject.

'Lungs' is the focus in the organ facet of the subject.

'Tuberculosis' is the focus in the problem facet of the subject.

'X-ray treatment' is the focus in the hand facet of the subject.

Medicine (Basic subject)

Organ facet	Problem facet	Handling facet
(Human Parts, e.g. head, problem face, ears, eyes, nose lungs, etc.)	(Types of diseases affecting human body, e.g. Morphology, Physiology, disease, T.B., etc.)	(Methods of treatment of different problems, e.g. symptoms, diagnosis, Pathology Therapeutics, X-ray, Electro-therapy, etc.)

Example from Library Science (Facet)

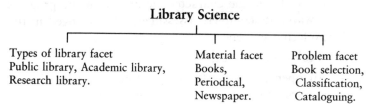

Library Science

Types of library facet	Material facet	Problem facet
Public library, Academic library, Research library.	Books, Periodical, Newspaper.	Book selection, Classification, Cataloguing.

Hence, facet is a part of compound subject. While focus denotes an isolate forming part of a particular facet.

15.2 Facet

— A facet is a generic term used to denote any component be it a basic subject or an isolate of a compound subject (C Prolegomena. Cr7).

— Facet is a generic term used to denote a component of a CdS- compound subject, such as a BC, or an isolate.

Array

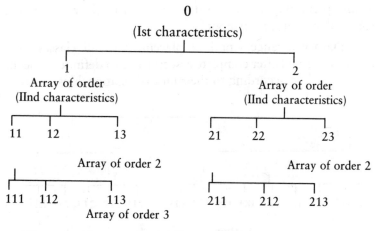

These are the arrays of different orders.

Single characteristics bear equal relation

Example: 11, 12, 13 — a group of coordinate classes.

or

21, 22, 23 — a group of coordinate classes.

— Array means, 'The classes derived from a universe on a basis of a single characteristic at one in the progress towards its complete assessment and arranged in the preferred sequence'.

(Prolegomena. CEI)

— An open array — 'An array of classes, admitting of extrapolation' is known as an open array.

Main Class

2

New classes   New classes
can be accommodated   can be
                                                     accommodated

It is a continuous process.

15.3 Filiatory Sequence

The term filiatory is derived from the word 'filial' which means 'pertaining to a son or daughter bearing the relation' of a son or daughter, an offshoot.

Filiatory arrangement is a placement of all classes of a universe derived after complete assortment in a definite sequence in a single line according to their mutual relationships.

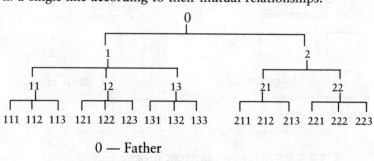

0 — Father

1, 2 — Two living sons

Son No. 1 has three children (sons)	11, 12, 13
Son No. 2 has two children (sons)	21, 22
Now Grandson 11 has three children	111, 112, 113
The other Grandson 12 has three children	121, 122, 123

The third Grandson 13 has three children   131, 132, 133
Similarly the case of grandsons 21, 22
— These classes are originated form.

15.4 Facet Analysis

Facet analysis means the breaking down a subject into facet.

Vickery: "First analysis first groups the terms into categories — king, state, property, reaction, operation device and so on — and then arranges terms within each category into the form of a classificatory map."

Ranganathan: "Facet analysis is a mental process by which the possible trains of characteristics which can form the basis of classification of a subject and exact measure in which the attributes concerned are incident in each facet of the subject are determined."

Metcalfe: "Facet analysis seems to mean either what has been called subject analysis of particular documents, as a step to their synthetic representation by so called class or code numbers, or it means the analysis of the subject field to discover a basis for its classification, whether enumerative or analytic synthetic."

Palmer and Wells: "Facet analysis means the analysis of the specific subject into the facets produced by the application of different characteristics."

Advantages:

1. The prior analysis of the material into facet is the most valuable intellectual aid to the classificationists. Subjects are organised in a class relationship in a subject matter. Classificationist aids clear thinking, reveals discrepancies in analysis and points the way to omissions in schedule.

2. The product of facet analysis is a set of schedule in which the terms are first grouped into more or less clearly defined facets and then within each facet, arranged in a class order. The classifier finds it easier to spot compound terms in a title and to factorise them appropriately.

3. If the index is based upon generic relations, which are clearly displayed in faceted schedules, these objects are attained most readily.

15.5 Principles of Facet Sequence

It is really a problem to decide a 'facet formula' within each class. Formula should be based on:

(a) Need of the user.

(b) Reflect the interests of the user.

(c) It should be strictly followed.

(d) Absolute consistency is maintainted.

Example: Classification of manuscripts in public library in India in 1965.

Public library – MSS – Classification — India —1965.

1. The subject factors should precede the form of presentation of the information and document.

Example: *Dictionary of Applied Psychology*

Psychology – Applied — Dictionary

2. Means should be subordinated to ends since most subject fields reflect some kind, the purpose of which is ultimately the production of something.

3. If it is a compound subject, the part is dependent on the 'whole', thus giving a citation order "Whole – part".

4. More concrete element should always be cited before less concrete ones.

Ranganathan has given following principles to determine the sequence of facets:

(a) Commodity—Raw material—Transformation principle. The commodity facet will always be taken as a manifestation of personality.

Example: Textiles—Yarn—Cotton—Spinning.

(b) Wall–Picture Principle—It examines the sequence between two manifestations of 'energy', like 'Disease and Cure.'

Example: Medicine — Disease (E) – Cure (E).

(c) Act and — Action — Actor — Tool principle — Facets are arranged in sequence.

Example: Medicine-Lungs-Disease— Tubercular Bacillus.

Cow-Calf–Principle— Even an unwanted calf cannot be sold. Cow and Calf are kept together, though they are separate entities.

Example: (Design) (Electrical Engg.) (Engg.) (Lift) Engineering — Electrical Engg. — Lift—Design.

5. Whole Organ Principle: This principle arranges the sequence of two isolates.

Example: History — India — President.

15.6 Telescoping Facet

When different facets belonging to schedules in an idea plane appear to be telescoped into a single schedule in the notational plane, it is called "telescoping facet". In other words, presentation of schedules of all the levels if they formed a single schedule. Different levels of the same fundamental category exist in one or the same round. It is useful :

(a) The naming of different level 1 and level 2 in the schedules while naming relatively to one another. New subject may turn up calling for a new level of facets.

(b) If a subject does not present some intermediate levels, the isolate number belonging to them need not find a place in the class number.

Example:

7 Industrial relation in first sector of 9 'personal management' of (E) of main class Economics.

97	Industrial Relation	Least concrete sector
971	Moral Maintenance	of 9
976	Arbitration	
978	Settlement	

979 A	Stained Relation	⎫
979 D	Strike	More concrete sector
979 W	Lockout	of 97
97 B	Employee	⎫ Still more concrete sector
97 K	National Trade Union	of 97
97 W	Employer Union	⎭

15.7 Telescoping of Arrays

Telescoping of arrays means the presentation of the isolates obtained on the basis of the different characteristics in the same array as the one presenting the characteristics themselves as quasi Isolates. Sector notation is advantageous to telescope the isolates based on different quasi isolates in the same facet and present them in a single schedule as shown in notational plane.

Example:

D9L 22 Diesel Engine
1 By starter
6 Electrical
9m Air-cooled   Foci in (P)
(A) By purpose
(K) Diesel engine for ship

If the subject presents two or more of these isolates, the isolate numbers are linked with the help of superimposition device, i.e. connecting symbol hyphen (-) is used to link these isolates.

Example:

Class number with fanned out isolates:

D9 L 22	Electricity
D9 L 22, 6	Electrically started diesel engines
D9 L 229 m	Air-cooled diesel engines
D9 L22m, 6	Electrically started air-cooled diesel engines.

16

Chain Indexing

It is a mechanical method to drive subject headings or subject indexing entries from the class number of the document.

Ranganathan never accepted the "marking and parking" role of classification. His object about the role of classification was:

(i) To analyse the subject of the document into its fundamental component.

(ii) To synthesise these components in a logical order in a classificatory language.

(iii) To be coexhaustively expressive of the specific subject of the documents.

(iv) To make on the basis of chain indexing.

Its logic may be stated as:

(i) It is an analytical and synthetic scheme of classification.

(ii) It (classification scheme) has a structured notational system.

(iii) It is used as in the coextensive representation of the subject.

(iv) Then retranslation of the class number is done using the schedule of the same classification scheme.

(v) Then it will give a nearly structured formulation of subject.

The job of chain indexing is not a job of indexer, but a classifier.

Indexer status and classifier has left or finished subject headings which are derived to provide alphabetical approach to the subject of document.

— Cataloguing supplement the work of classification through alphabetical index entries derived mechanically by chain procedure.

— It is a symbiosis of classification and cataloguing. (Ranganathan)

16.1 Coextensiveness—A Way Out

Name of subject, called—class number in notational plane.

Subject heading, called—class number in verbal plane.

— Chain procedure is a device to drive subject headings from class number.

— In other words, it is called expression of ideas and is also called discourse (device).

— Discourse may be an information source of users query.

Class number

|

(Process) Device (Discourse)

|

Subject headings (Machine subjects)

|

Used for subject indexing in alphabetical index entries

|

It is source of Information Retrieval system (Basis of indexing system)

The problem involves: To identify and specify coextensively the subjects of discourses:

(a) Subject of information Science ⎤ in the form of subject
                                    ⎟   headings.
(b) Subjects of user's query   ⎟
    as basis of subject indexing.   ⎦

1. It is difficult for the user to:
   (a) Perceive,
   (b) Precisely, and
   (c) Expressively—the subject of his interest.
2. Language problem.
3. Information to the conveyed.
4. Particular component theoretically.
5. Information scientists have less knowledge of the interest
   of the users.

Hence, non-coextensiveness in the discourse is a problem in
an indexing system.

Remedy of the problem of non-coextensiveness may provide
access on the indexing file to:

(a) Subjects of greater extension which also include the
    subjects of user's interest.
(b) Subjects of a greater intension which also contain a
    substantial portion of the subject of user's interest.
(c) Subjects which are related to the subject of interest to
    the user.

    Index file providing access to subject —
    (i)   of greater extension,
    (ii) of greater intention,
    (iii) also to related subjects, and
    (iv) also specific subjects.
          — is a better tool for information retrieval.

16.2 Logic behind Chain Indexing

Ranganathan had in mind a classified order of documents
and a classified catalogue to approach the documents.

A classified arrangement would necessarily reflect a particular pattern of ramification of a subject and help to provide approach to the subject from a particular point of view. This was determined mainly by the characteristic chosen at each level of division in the classification scheme.

Chain procedure is an alternative approach to frame subject headings.

"Chain procedure is a procedure for deriving class index entry from a class number, in a more or less mechanical way. It is used to derive class index subject entry, subject analytical and see also subject entries in dictionary catalogue."

In other words, chain procedure is a semi-mechanical method to derive class index entries (subject word entries) from a chain drawn out at successive sub-division of a class number.

16.3 Steps in Chain Indexing

There are eleven steps involved in chain indexing:

(a) Specific subject of a document is determined with the help of the title of the document, its table of contents and by a perusal of the text carefully. By analysing the subject, contents of a documents are arrived at its specific subject.

(b) Naming of the specific subject of the document expressively in the natural language in terms as decided (expressive name of subject).

(c) Representation of the name of specific subject in terms of its fundamental components (name of subject in kernel terms). It is done by removing all the auxiliary words from the title.

(d) Determination of the category or status or role of each fundamental component according to the set of postulates and principles formulated for this purpose (analysed name of subject).

(e) Transformation of the analysed name of subject by rearranging, if necessary, the fundamental components, according to a few additional postulates and principles formulated for the purpose of governing the syntax. (transformed name-of-subject)

(f) Standardization of each term in the transformed name-of-subject (name of subject in standard terms). If the name of subject is not in accordance with the standard terms used in preferred scheme of classification, it should be replaced by its equivalent standard terms, as given in the schedule. If the terms in the schedule are not current, help of the sources or a glossary of the subject may be taken.

(g) Determination of each of the links of the chain in which the subject denoted by the name-of-subject-in-standard form is the last link (determination of under link). Representation of the class number in the form of a chain in which each link consists of two parts— the class number and its translation. It is done as follows:

(i) Make the first link from the first digit.

(ii) Make the second link out two digits and so on, up to the last link (link occurring last in the chain produced by a class number) which is to be made of all digits.

(iii) Write the links one below the other in succession.

(iv) Write against each link its translation into natural language.

(v) Join the "-" sign of each link with that of the next succeeding link by a downward arrow, if necessary.

(h) Determination of the different kinds of links, such as, sought link, unsought link, false link and missing link (determination of kinds of link). False link is that which is not a class number. It does not represent a subject with a definite name. A link is false link if it ends with a connecting symbol or digit representing time itself. Unsought link is that which ends with a part of the isolate focus in a class number or represents a subject or which reading material is not likely to be produced or sought or which is not likely to be looked up by any reader seeking material on the specific subject. Missing link is a link in a chain with gap corresponding to a missing isolate in the chain. Sought link is that link through which a user approaches his document. It is neither a false link nor an unsought link.

(i) Derivation of subject heading from each of the sought links in the chain according to a set of rules formulated to suit the purpose at hand (derivation of subject headings).

The procedure for deriving subject heading is to start from the terms of the last sought link and proceed towards the terms of upper link, in a reverse rendering process.

(j) Construction of specific heading for specific subject entry or subject reference entry is to be made with the minimum number of terms of such upper links as are necessary and sufficient to make the subject heading meaningful and individualised. Each term in the heading or sub-heading is to be a single noun in normative case except when a qualifying adjective is necessary as in "Digestive System" or " Social Science".

(k) The specific subject entries, subject reference entries and entries for cross references should be merged and arranged in a single alphabetical sequence.

"Chain indexing is a procedure for deriving alphabetical subject headings through digit by digit interpretation of a class number of a document. A class number generates a series of link forming a chain."

Example: =   0111, 1 M 56, 1

0   =   Literature (Sought link)

01   =   Tectonic, Literature (Unsought link)

011   =   Indo-European, Literature (Unsought link)

0111   =   English, Literature (Sought link)

0111,   =   False link

0111, 1	=	Poetry, English, Literature (Sought link)
0111,1M56	=	False link
0111,1M56,1	=	Mr. Whitman by Pullen (Stanley T. poetry)

/

Last link/Lower link

Connecting digits are false link

Subject represented but not sought by users is Unsought link. Rest are Sought link and they convey meaning directly related to the document under difference and users are likely to approach this document through them.

Hence, Mr. Whitman, Pallm (Stanley T.) 0111,1M56, 1

Whitman, Poetry, English	0111,1M 56
Poetry, English, Literature	0111,1
English literature	0111
Literature	0

/

Specific subject of the document, and rest of the links are of greater extension. Practical guide to colon classification 2:51'N3:

2	=	Library Science (Sought link)
2:	=	False link
2:5	=	Technical treatment, Library Science (Unsought link)
2:51	=	Classification, Library Science (Sought link)
2:51N3	=	Colon classification (Sought link).

The subject headings, generated by the Sought links are as follows:

Colon classification, Library Science	2:51N3
Classification, Library Science	2:51
Library Science	2

Reference Entries for Specific Subject: In the alphabetical indexes, where physical collocation is not there, reference entries are made to provide direction to the specific subject headings.

— Library Science
See also Colon classification
— Classification, Library Science
See Colon classification.

16.4 Merits of Chain Indexing

(a) The classifier analyses the subject of the document to have a structural formulation of the subject as its class number. The indexer starts from this stage and retranslates the class number to provide alphabetical approach through class index entries. Chain indexing thus saves the duplication of work.

(b) Chain indexing is based on the classification number and the terminology given in the schedules. It is, therefore, semi-mechanical as also a speedy procedure.

(c) Irrespective of the scheme of classification, subject headings or class index entries can be derived from class number with the help of chain indexing. Though this procedure is more suited to the analytico-synthetic scheme of classification, yet it has adaptability with different notational schemes. Mill has also shown that chain indexing can be applied with ease to any classification scheme whose notation symbols indicate the subordination of each step of division.

(d) For a string having four components, only four subject headings are made according to chain indexing, though the permutation of four terms would have given 24 headings. This system thus brings in term endorse economy.

(e) Chain indexing provides alternative approach to the classified file through reverse rendering. It is helpful to the users in retrieving their information.

(f) DRTC has found chain procedure fully amendable to computerisation. Programmes were successfully written to generate subject headings both from class number and feature heading necessary for guides, gangway guides, bay guides, shelf guides, etc. in the consistency way.

16.5 Limitations of Chain Indexing

1. Out of the subject headings derived through chain indexing for documents, the last link is specific and others represent broader subjects.

(i) Last link heading will serve these readers who search for specific subjects headings.

(ii) Other headings serve the readers who search for general reading, i.e. particular heading.

(iii) Unrelated and unwanted links or so-called parts of the headings are rejected as they are of no use for readers.

2. Some empty links are also derived in the chain procedure; these are generic entries. Such entries make noise or confuse the researcher working in highly specialised field.

3. Chain indexing depends on class number. Hence, its efficiency depends on the scheme of classification. If scheme of classification is not efficient, the chain indexing will not derive the proper subject headings and it will not serve the purpose of the users.

4. There is also a problem of false or Unsought link as they are unrepresented in the chain.

Some Expert Observation:

— The idea of chain procedure originated in 1930.

— The work on the subject index made up of the unit terms was started on the basis of the contemporary edition of colon classification.

— The procedure was first applied to the Dewey's 'Decimal classification class numbers'.

— Rules were changed when applied by Ranganathan to the CC class number.

— It was also proved that chain procedure could be applied to the class numbers constructed according to any scheme of classification.

According to many experts:

(a) Chain procedure was a definite, impersonal, mechanical and adjective method. It can be applied to any classification scheme.

(b) Some modifications are required in regard to complex subjects.

(c) Chain procedure is a mean for transferring the relations in the synthetic system into the cross reference entries of an alphabetical index.

(d) Its successful application is possible to DC class numbers.

(e) Mill support Palmer and Well. He says whatever notation may be, chain procedure can be applied to all major schemes.

(f) Chain procedure is not much disturbed by the defect in classification scheme. It is a useful procedure to determine the keymode (Mill).

(g) All defects may be solved if applied to DC.

Chain procedure is justified and is a significant approach / step towards mechanical subject indexing in a classified catalogue.

Improvements: Neelmeghan has suggested as follows :

1. Rotation of components of the string, instead of dropping the components one by one.

2. Rotation will keep all headings complete.

3. There should be breaking point where common isolate idea begins.

16.6 Adoption of Chain Indexing by BNB

Chain indexing system is one of the greatest contributions to the field of subject cataloguing. It was used by British National Bibliography for two decades. Over the last 25 years chain procedure has been considerably amended and improved.

The 4th edition of CCC (1958) contained a special terminology of chain procedure and tight it up with the special terminology of a synthetic classification. After applying chain procedure for BNB, E.J. Coats has produced a more modified structure of headings in subject catalogue. He has analysed the chain procedure and explained chain procedure indexing reflecting the modulated structure of classification scheme tends to represent complex ideas by means of elementary combined terms, rather than by single complex terms; because of this, the coverage of subject relationship signalled by a classified catalogue supported by collocation of terms in a chain procedure. Index is probably greater than that produced by any alternative method of indexing.

Demerits

1. It does not provide detailed rules of direct application except a few guidelines to apply the chain procedure.

2. Cataloguer has no liberty to use his knowledge and experience to decide which Cross Reference Index entry to prepare that will be correct.

3. Chain procedure cannot be applied to the scheme of classification having no canon of hospitality in array and chain.

4. Universe of knowledge in a changing procedure and classification should be changed accordingly.

Chain procedure is class number based and is conventional. It was experienced that it should be made possible to apply the chain procedure in corporating classified catalogue system in the Dictionary Catalogue System.

Analytico-Synthetic Scheme of Classification

This is the classification which aims at breaking down subject into constituent elements, and then resynthesising them in a consistent manner. Ranganathan introduced colon classification which is entirely based on analytico-synthetic principles. This aims at the following :

(a) Analysing first the subject field into constituent elements or facets.

(b) Constructing the class number by synthesis.

(c) Readymade class numbers are not assigned to topics.

(d) It has certain standard unit schedules.

(e) Standard unit schedules correspond to the standard pieces of Meccano apparatus.

(f) Many different objects may be constructed by facet analysis.

(g) This aim can also be achieved by combining the classes in different unit scheduled in assigning permutation and combinations.

(h) The function of colon is like nut and bolts in a Meccano set.

(i) Colon classification can be compared to a Meccano set consisting of slotted strips, wheels, screws, nuts and pieces of string.

(j) With a few digits, called the alphabets, an endless variety of words, phrases, sentences, paragraphs can be made.

In other words, the postulates make classification scheme analytico-synthetic. These provide for —

(i) Fundamental categories.

(ii) Phase analysis.

(iii) Facet analysis involving.

(iv) Round analysis.

(v) Level analysis.

There are some general principles for Zone-analysis. This provides standard procedure for construction schedules of isolates belonging to different facets. The work of classifying any subject, compounded and embodied in any graphical form for communication, has been thus reduced to five stages:

(i) Analysing the subject into its ultimate phases and the facets in the different phases and naming the isolates in each facet.

(ii) Rearranging the names of the isolates so as to conform to the syntax of the classificatory language adopted.

(iii) Changing the name of each isolate in to the standard terminology.

(iv) Transculating the name of isolate in each facet into isolate number with the aid of the schedule for the facet and the devices applicable to it.

(v) Synthesising the basic class number and the different isolate numbers into the class number with the aid of the connecting symbols.

A scheme of classification work in these five stages is known as Analytico-Synthetic Classification. Work in the first two stages is entirely in idea plane. Work in second and third stages is entirely in idea plane. Work in fourth stage is both verbal and notational plane.

Even in enumerative scheme, some analysis of idea plane is necessary but it is not guided by standard procedures. The second, third and fourth stages are not distinguishable. Perhaps they may be said not to occur at all. Having formulated the subject in same way, it is merely a question of 'Hit or Miss' with the aid of the systematic schedule and alphabetical index.

Arrangement: The first use is to preserve a preferred helpful sequence among known specific subjects without the necessity for re-examining their sequence. In other words, the first use was mechanisation of arrangement.

17.1 Exploration

A properly designed classification should be able to assign to a newly formed specific subject such a class number as would place it among already known specific subjects, in a totally helpful position. This implies firstly the existence of appropriate vacant numbers of the reception of new subjects and secondly the vacant number suggests the certainty of the corresponding new subjects. Facet and Phase analysis, including fundamental categories, round —levels and zone analysis and the use of Seminal mnemonics, should be practiced intensively to get the fullest benefit of this, the second use of literary classification.

An analytic-synthetic classification scheme can be helpful in the promotion of international communication and translation from one natural language to another.

(a) **Emotional Sphere:** Classification belongs to the intellectual plane, and it cannot directly eliminate emotion of any kind nor can classification help in the international communication of emotions.

(b) **Trans-Intellectual Sphere:** There are certain ineffable elements in the experiences and thought of men, which cannot be communicated by an external means, but can only be experienced by each one independently. Poetry, painting, sculpture, music and other fine arts and symbolism of all kinds can only communicate it potentially.

The ineffability of experience in this sphere is traceable to its being trans-intellectual classification should abstain from analysing such ineffable elementary of trans-intellectual experience. It should treat them as a whole. This is purpose of classic device in classification.

(c) **Intellectual Sphere:** International economy requires that the output of research should promptly serve to all concerned, even when it is in its nascent state. The diversity of language militates against it. It will be a long time before the terminology can be made uniform. A term in a natural language, used by the creator of the thought, usually produces in the mind of others several unintended associations and thus blurs the image of the thoughts.

(d) **Transformer language:** It is true that a well-designed scientifically constructed analytic-synthetic classification can be of considerable help in international communication and in the communication of ascent thought within a language. If the scheme of classification is sufficiently equipped with the mnemonics of high potency to form foci, facet–formula with provision for optional facets to express all possible manifestation of the chosen fundamental categories as facets and phase formula with distinctive symbols for all possible relations between different subjects, every new specific subject will be born with its own class number in its pocket as it were. The class number will indicate to an enquirer the entry valuable to him, and he may ask for that alone to be translated into his own language.

17.2 Structure and Development

1. **Banyan Tree Analogy:** Analytico-synthethic scheme is comparable to a banyan tree with immunerable branches, sub-branches (facets) divided in different directions, and with some branches divided downward and striking roots (phases) and themselves becoming secondary stems.

On the other hand, the structure of the schedule of an analytico-synthetic scheme of classification is also different from that enumerative one. It consists of several independent schedules.

2. **Meccano Analogy:** In colon classification the standard unit schedule of an analytico-synthetic scheme is compared to the standard pieces of steps, wheels in Meccano set. By combining these standard pieces in different ways, many different objects can be constructed. So also by combining the isolate in the different unit schedules in a prescribed manner, the class number for function of connecting symbols is likely that of bolts and nuts in the Meccano set.

3. **Medical Analogy:** Some have compound and enumerative scheme of classification to patent medicine. The doctor has no doubt to make some diagnosis, but than he has to choose the medicine from among the readymade patent one. On the other hand, an analytico-synthetic classification scheme has been compared to compound medicine. The doctor diagnoses each patient thoroughly, and then writes out a prescription to meet the diverse indication of the diagnoses, and also decide their suitability to each individual case. He measures each drugs and synthesises them with necessary secondary substances.

So the classification analysis is an idea plane corresponding to diagnose. The synthesis is notational plane that corresponds to the compounding, —each subject gets its own individualising class number.

4. **Language Analogy:** An analytico-synthetic scheme of classification is like a dictionary of words taken along with grammar of the language. It enables to express any idea as and when it occurs to the user. In the same manner it is possible to construct class number for any subject by analysing it into its ultimate phases, facets and foci translating each of these with the dictionary, and then forming a class number by synthesis.

5. **Structure of Schedule:** It is many schedules, some common to all subjects, some common to some subjects, some special to individual subjects, some are even special to individual isolates in the different facets of one and the same subjects. There is no readymade schedule. It constructs few hundred short schedules of isolates in addition of short schedules of basic class.

6. **Constituent verses Composite Terms:** An analytico-synthetic classification takes the responsibility to fix the name of

the class in a natural language. It restricts itself to the task of naming the isolates in the various facets. It restricts itself to the fundamental constituent terms. It leaves the desired composite terms to the care of individual classifier and reference books.

Development: The development of analytico synthetic classification consists in adding to the number of its schedules will be called for by new rounds and new levels of the fundamental categories involved in micro thought getting embodied from time to time. Its schedule is ever growing the growth of schedule length will be linear.

17.3 Autonomy to Classifier

Many classes, now unknown and unknowable, will be known and will call for a helpful place and an appropriate class number from time to time in the future. A new class may represent a new facet, not found scheduled in the scheme, or a facet of it. Though already found scheduled, may present a focus not listed in the schedule. Then two things may happen. It may call for a new focus in an array already scheduled, or it may call for new array to be formed.

In enumerative scheme, classifier has to depend on classificationist to find the number for a new class. He cannot create it by itself. But in an analytico-synthetic scheme, the classificationist would have given rules of procedure to analyse the subject in idea plane, to arrange the resulting facets in a definite sequence and then to look up for a schedule for translation into numbers.

There are other rules implementing the canon of classification, particularly those relating to mnemonics, will help in putting up of a new schedule, or the extension of existing array or the lengthening of an existing chain in the schedule—whatever is demanded by new subject. Classifier can create a new number by himself.

The colon classification gives the autonomy to the classifier in an appreciable measure.

17.4 Design of Analytico-Synthetic Classification Scheme

1. Classification:

(a) Idea plane (grouping).

(b) Verbal plane(Arrangement of groups).

(c) Notational plane (Representation of groups in ordinal numbers).

(a) **Idea plane:** Grouping of existence of Universe

    (i) Grouping of concrete or conceptual.

    (ii) Grouping of things or ideas.

Single characteristics— Train of characteristics and in sequence.

(b) **Verbal plane:**

Classification is arranging group.

Group is arranged in one or other of several sequences. Sequence equals the number of permutations of the groups.

Arrangement in helpful sequence.

2. Facet and Phase Relation

3. Quality of Universe of Knowledge

(a) Multidimensional.

(b) Infinite.

(c) Continuous.

(d) Dynamic.

(e) Turbulent.

(f) Postulation approach.

(g) Basic class and isolates.

(i) Main class and (BC).

(j) Length of the base (Notation).

(k) Superimposition.

18

Outlines of Library Classification

The collection of books in big quantity always creates problem of arrangement when specific works are likely to be sought by persons other than those who collected the work. The owner of private library can lay his hands on finding his book because of no proper arrangement. He also takes a long time to search his book. But Librarian is a 'Host' to the 'Readers' who have no leisure time for searching their books out of huge collection of a library. Librarian must group his books to meet the needs of his reader. He must use the principle of orderly arrangement to reduce the cumulative loss of time to successive readers.

In ancient times when books were few and readers were limited, the arrangement of books was according to colour, size and author. Any grouping is better than none, but some better grouping based on some systems and principles are always better. The size of book tells us nothing more than its dimensions, and the colour nothing more than the hues of the binding materials. These two criterias are ephemeral. The authorship can imply other qualities but to a limited degree; it tells us the probable subject of a book. If he/she is a known mathematician, the book probably belongs to mathematics. But all such extrinsic qualities fail to help us much and we must seek our useful arrangement elsewhere.

Every book has some permanent qualities.

1. It has an author.

2. It has a title.

3. It has a subject.

Author arrangement is related to a permanent feature of a book but it is useless to a reader looking for subject. Author arrangement can only properly respond to an author approach to books.

Title of book is much less stable than its authors name, since title arrangement is arrangement by the accident of the first word.

The ordinary reader needs his book by author but under a specific subject. Subject is a direct or indirect approach of a book. It is intelligent to anticipate this by arranging the books to meet it. Scientists and technicians want to know what is being done in their line of work by others. Subject arrangement breaks down into many small groups, and provides the reader a general idea of a subject with which his author was occupied in the book he is seeking. However, a useful exercise might be to tabulate all the pro and cons of each method, assigning value to them and then to draw up a balance sheet.

What do we mean by subject? We mean a specific subject which is that division of knowledge which exactly comprehends all the major factors that go to its making.

Example: 1

History of Steam Engine =

(1) Steam Engine.

(2) History or Historical approach.

Examle: 2

Unemployment in India in 1960 =

(1) Unemployment (specific subject).

(2) India (geographical place).

(3) 1960 (period).

When we have decided a subject from the title and the author, the book is to be arranged along with other subjects, if we isolate minor subject like prime numbers, fractions, etc. to arrange books by their specific subjects. Consider the subjects, sun, moon, planets, earth, solar system. They are all parts of Astronomy. They are put together based on their relations and helpful order, as a reader studying Astronomy or its various aspects may find his book in between these subjects and specific subjects. We must try to arrive at as helpful an order as possible, and arrange our books in related groups in the way that the generality of readers will use them. Alphabetical order does not seem to suffice. Some other order, more closely related to the subjects themselves, must be brought.

Order to be Selected

We have to select one order which is proper for arrangement. The arrangement should be:

(i) commonly accepted;

(ii) used for longest period;

(iii) used by greatest number of readers;

(iv) according to the special grouping of subjects;

(v) to save the time;

(vi) to save the energy; and

(vii) to save the money.

In view of the above, the system of classification should be such which is most useful to search the book without waiting unnecessarily for more time and putting in labour. It should be easy to understand by the readers.

18.1 Left to Right

If books are arranged according to an order, it should be arranged from left to right, which is convenient to all readers and is within their approach. Left to right order also relates to the religious order and common man's choice. The reader also likes to search readily just that part of a shelf of books which seems appropriate to his needs, and to move left to right to the exact spot helped by the order.

18.2 Helpful Order

This is the order which displays subjects in such a way that a person approaching a group of subjects at any point is led by the order itself to the specific subject he needs. There are three aspects to be considered:

  (i) observing the habit of reader;
 (ii) the subject the reader's need; and
(iii) other related subjects of the specific subject of the choice of the reader.

B.I. Palmer and A.J. Wells says:

"The helpful sequence can be defined as that which displays subjects in such a way that a person approaching a group of subjects at any point is led by the order itself to the specific subject he needs."

It means :

observing the habit of readers;
meeting the demand of the readers.

There are propositions that:

1. Most of the people do not think in terms of specific subjects.

2. Most of the peoples think in terms of general subject.

3. Readers require other related material of the subject.

4. Many people cannot accurately define a specific subject until actually confronted with it.

5. Many specific subjects are only to be found with material for a more general nature.

Therefore, an order which itself leads to a specific subject sought is followed by the specific subject itself. No matter what is point of approach, demand is a system which arranges a subject in order of decreasing extension. Specificity is a relative mater. We have to fix an order — the order which gives increasing specificity, no matter how complex the subject, and what arrangement it has.

It may be explained as under:

1. The general treated generally = Introduction of Medicine.
2. The general treated specially   = Surgery, a Guide.
3. The special treated generally   = Stomach : a Handbook.
4. The special treated specially   = Surgery of the Stomach.

18.3 Terms of Classification

The arrangement of books needs some name which can represent the thoughts and themes of the book. Such name given to the book is called 'term'. Such terms are subject-groups. We can refer these terms conveniently. This is the reason we call some books on Science, Commerce, Arts, Economics, Law, etc. The names thus given are called the terms of classification.

Such terms obviously differ in scope and this variation is called the extension and intention of the subjects. A wide subject will have wider extension or wide area of knowledge. The subject which have little contents have little intention. As we move down from wider to narrow subjects, terms are denoting concepts of increasing smaller extension. But as they are dealing with more and more definite subject, we know more and more about them.

Example =   500   — Science (wide extension).

510   — Mathematics (narrow extension than science).

But both are related to each other as shown from abstract number 5.

Hence, the subject of smaller extension becomes more and more definite in meaning because the intention of the subject increases.

Relationship among Subjects

When we decide terms of the subject, the next step is to put them in a group — one group of one characteristics.

Example

Group Ist line   = Science/Arts/Humanity.

Group IInd line   = Science = Mathematics, Chemistry, Physics, Technology, Zoology, Botany.

Group IIIrd line   = Mathematics = Algebra, Geometry, Arithmetic, Statistics.

Group IVth line   = Geometry = Line, plane, three dimensions, four dimensions.

Group Vth line   = Three dimensions = Configuration, surface of second degree, cubic, quartic, curve in space, knot.

Example = Building work

Building work = Bricklaying and masonry

Bricklaying and masonry = tiling and carpentry and so on.

It is possible to look at this from a different viewpoint, however, and to arrive at the same conclusion. Suppose we have a good number on 'building' and we wish to break them in groups bringing together to make a whole. There is no difference so far as fundamentals are concerned, but there is a difference of approach. There are two rules for practical work:

1. Rule of thumb and corrects his errors as he goes.
2. (For theoretical work) observing the results of the efforts of the practical man and following the general rules.

Practically:

(a) Shelves the groups as they occur.

(b) Labels each in some such way.

      = MASONRY, CARPENTRY, TILING, PLANNING, PLASTERING, etc.

Theoretically:

(a) Writing down the terms denoting the whole contents of the collection.

(b) After some cogitation adds 'divide by the building operation'.

(c) List the groups into which divide the book at later stage.

However, the efforts are:

1. Break down the books into right sort of groups.
2. Take into account (or correlate) as many qualities of the subjects of the books as possible.
3. There are so many aspects to any subject.

The resultant divisions may be listed as under :

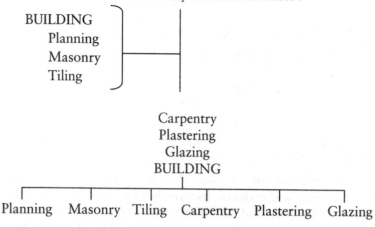

BUILDING
  Planning
  Masonry
  Tiling

                Carpentry
                Plastering
                Glazing
                BUILDING

Planning   Masonry   Tiling   Carpentry   Plastering   Glazing

The genealogical tree form shows:

1. Each of the operations listed is of equal rank in the division.
2. Each drives directly from the general task of 'building'.
3. None of them is subordinate to each of them.
4. Hence, they are coordinate groups.
5. They are equal in rank.
6. We can see all such subjects at a glance.

Now see whether all these coordinated subjects are put in helpful sequence. No doubt any given number of objects can be arranged in $1 \times 2 \times 3......$ x and this gives a vast number of possible orders.

There are two preferential order :

1. Alphabetical order, or
2. One based on the order in which the operations are applied (to the actual erection of a building).

The arrangement in library involves two steps:

1. The breaking down of a class into a number of coordinate divisions by the consistent application of a given principle.

2. The assembling of the resultant series of coordinate divisions into most useful order.

There are four possible orders in array:

Canonical (complying with custom)
Evolutionary
Spatial contiguity
Categorical (*ad hoc* order).

Hence, if we go by above example, when the groups exhausted, the other characteristic may be the material of building and divide them into smaller groups.

The process of division demands that we take one characteristic and exhaust its possibilities, then take another and do likewise, and so till we reach the smallest groups convenient for our use. At each step we shall get an array of divisions coordinate with one another, and these must be put into helpful order each time.

Helpful order

Helpful order is to arrange like subjects with like and according to the needs of the workers within a given field. We begin with a species and assign it to its genus. The classifier assigns books to various divisions and puts on each book the symbol appropriate to its subject.

Example:

Pre-School child
Elementary stage (5-11)
Secondary stage (11-18)
University stage (18-22)
Adult stage (22).

Problem

Curriculum
Teaching methods
Provision of buildings.

This process of division by characteristics is fundamental to all classification schemes. Enumerative classification scheme lists composit subjects built up from a number of basic ideas. Faceted classifications list the basic terms.

Enumerative scheme

> Religion: General
> > Founders of religious
> > Sacred books.
>
> Christianity
> > Christ
> > Bible.
>
> Mohammedanism
> > Mohammed
> > Koran.

18.4 Faceted Classification Scheme

Religion	(Religion involved)	(Activity involved)
	Christianity	Founder
	Mohammedanism	Sacred books.

Here, we find that all characteristics chosen as the basis of division are related to those qualities which are practical manifestations of five fundamental concepts. These are time, space, energy, matter and personality. The first four are concept basic to science, while fifth is the quality which underlies the infinite variety of things. Just as there are infinite varieties of colours, but only four are primary, so there is an infinite variety of subjects, but only five fundamental concepts.

Example 1

Consider the subject 'ploughing' name as operation in Agriculture.

Operation of Ploughing = Agriculture + Energy

Divide each side into its component parts. (Operation) of (ploughing) = (Agriculture) + (Energy) we get – Operation = Energy (equation 1).

It is completely general concept and unrelated to any particular subject.

Example 2

Specific subject 'History of subject'.

(History) of the (Geographical area) (England) = History (space), Geographical area = space.

Time	= It is a period division.
Space	= It is a geographical area.
Energy	= It represents problems, made of work or approach.
Matter	= It represent the physical form in various subjects.
Personality	= It represent the wholeness of any subject. (parts, kinds)

Phases and Phase Analysis

While we have divided the class or broken the class of books into groups by dividing them according to the manner or degree in which they pass a given attribute which we call the characteristic of division. Many a specific subject (or species) is abstracted from a more inclusive subject (or genus) by the application of characteristics.

Example: 'Methods of Hoeing Potatoes'.

1. Crop concerned.
2. Process of cultivation.

In most schemes the characteristics are not stated, but are implicit in the kinds of division enumerated. This makes the classifier's task most difficult.

1. Operation of characteristics
   Example: 'Woodworking'
   It may be divided in three ways –

Kinds of woodworking – carpentry, cabinet making, fretwork. (Personality)

By the material used — oak, ash, etc. (Matter)

By woodworking process. (Energy)

Woodworking	Kind (Personality)	Material (Matter)	Process (Energy)
	Rough	Hardwoods	Designing
	Fine	Softwoods	Marking out
	Decorative	Laminated	Shaping
		Woods	Smoothing

The divisions within each facet will be focused much more sharply.

General woodworking: The specific subject in woodworking is general. All the facets are present, yet none of them specifically – that its focus in each is diffuse, and subject, therefore is unfaceted.

Woodworking joints: In this subject the 'facet kind is considered vacant because diffuse, for the same reason, is a facet material. The subject is single-faceted.

Polishing oak cabinets: In this subject we can discern all three characteristics in action, as each of the facet is specified. The first is focused at 'cabinet-making', the second at 'oak', and the third is 'polishing'. The subject is triple-faceted.

Other examples

1. Mathematics for the biologist.
2. Chemical analysis of the soil.
3. Effects of war on the birthrate.
4. Psychotherapy and the Christian doctrine of man.

There are two subjects in each example. They belong to classes of 'mixed' subjects. Classification scheme does not provide for two mixed main-classes, except in few cases in few subjects in colon classification. We have the mind of man, through its instruments—books, bringing seemingly most incongruous bed-follows together. One of the two subjects thus thrown together is paramount.

1. The real subject is Mathematics, but it is treated with a bias towards biology. It deals with problems by using examples calculated to interest a biologist, and leaves out much of the mathematics which a biologist would not need.
2. It is used as a tool to study soils.
3. In this example we have social effect of war on one aspect of genetics. It is the one subject influencing another.
4. It demands a closer acquaintance with the specific book before we can decide which subject the author has made paramount. But it is in comparison of one subject with another.

The subjects Mathematics, Agriculture, Genetics and Religion are the paramount subjects and the subjects Biology, Chemical Analysis, War and Psychotherapy respectively are used to qualify these paramount subjects. In none of these cases does the secondary subject represent a facet of the paramount subjects. In every case the parts of these compound subjects would come from quite separate schedules of a general classification scheme. Indeed, in analyzing these compound subjects we can be said to move over from one part of the scheme to another, and each of the subjects represents a separate phase of analysis. We have called the paramount subject as the first phase of the compound subject, and the secondary subject as the second phase of the compound subject and having called them by this name, we perceive at once the likeness to the change of mode of division when we entered the phase of dividing a subject according to its form of presentation.

Thus, the specific subjects which go to make up a main class are not always completely described in terms of characteristics relating to the main class. On the contrary, they are often accretive, drawing to themselves parts of other main classes by way of relationship such as general, bias, influence, comparison and tool.

Example

'Teaching Methods in Elementary Education' = Single phased (Teaching methods, and children aged 5-11 years).

'Psychology for Teachers' = Two phased subject (Psychology and Education). Two areas of knowledge.

'Tomato-growing in green houses' = Single phased subject.

'Farming Arithmetic' = Two phased subject.

Now we can easily differentiate the facets and phases. Facets are closely related to the subject: they are the successive layers of which a subject is built up, like lamination in the piece of plywood. They are hard to prise apart. But phases are different: we can easily separate them one from another. They are loosely assembled.

Specific features

1. These are easily seen as additions to the subject.
2. There is difference between form of representation of a subject and various types of phase relations.
3. The use of form divisions is not a matter of assembly of two subjects but a way of presenting one.
4. It is called/described as dressing.
5. Symbols are used to indicate the form of representation.

18.5 Notation

Specific subjects are arranged systematically and formulated principles followed about the nature of this order. The names of main subject or main classes do not indicate in any way the position which they are intended to occupy in the order of the scheme of classification. It would be difficult to maintain a collection of books in systematic subject order according to a preconceived plan if the collection were not to be a museum piece. The order would be disturbed in use. The more valuable is the contents of the books and the nearer we had approximated to the most helpful order in their arrangement, the more they have been likely disturbed, because readers would have been finding what they wanted, and so removing books. We should obviously indicate the subject of each book quite clearly somewhere on it, and, going further, we should give it some sort of mark or symbol to indicate where in the sequence it should be inserted. Such symbols, signs alphabets and numerals which help in maintaining the sequence are called notations.

Notation is a device for mechanical arrangement and must be composed of written symbols whose order is defined. Generally two type of symbols are in use in most of the classification schemes: Arabic figures and Roman alphabets. A notation must consist of a series of digits which can be combined in a recognizable order. A digit can be defined as:

(i) any numeral – 0-9
(ii) any single sign of a series.

1. The digits of a notation do not require or possess a cardinal value; their only requirement is an ordinal

value. It is surely desirable that the chosen symbols should express order to the greatest number of people with the minimum of efforts. This implies that the number of arbitrary signs should be kept as small as possible, and they should be restricted to the representation of phenomena of less frequent occurrence.

2. The library user must be able to commit it to memory easily for his brief passage to the shelf in search of his book.

3. The reference assistant wants it to be easily written, for he will note each symbol down countless times. The cataloguing and accessions departments will want it to be easily typed, for the typewriter enters largely into our economy.

4. Arbitrary symbols are difficult to say. Quite ordinary symbols may prove awkward to say if they are present in two varieties, even though we may distinguish them readily at right. For example 'BaCFd' must be read as Capital 'B', small 'a', capital 'C' and 'F' and small 'd', which is unrhythmic and clumsy.

5. Shorter a notation, the easier it is remembered. They are more memorable if they are grouped and associated.

6. It is desirable that notation should be easy to read, write and type.

7. Notation should be brief. After all, it often has to go on the spine of the book, which is not always wide. It has to be written in good many records.

8. The shorter the notation the quicker the operation in writing.

9. Brevity in a notation must not be brought at the cost of order.

10. The fact is that the higher the degrees of intention of a class, the longer will be its notation.

11. Classification demands the representation of an infinite series of subjects by a finite series of symbols.

12. Notion should be made by sacrificing co-extensiveness with the subject of a book. Bliss has followed it in his classification scheme. Ranganathan prefers to seek co-extensiveness, even if it means a very long symbol.

Each separate symbol of any series is preferred as a sign. Each group of the same kind of symbol is called species of symbols.

(a) Letters have a large number of species, based on functions, design or origin. There are many types of symbols — Roman, Arabic numerals, Italic, Greek alphabets, upper and lower cases. These give us six species, each of which can, in turn, be accented, overlined or underlined to distinguish further species.

(b) Arbitrary signs have in theory, an infinite number of species. In point of fact, the only practicable ones are punctuation marks (some of which have a degree of recognized order) and mathematical signs (whose order has never become fixed). The former has been used by Bliss and latter by UDC.

(c) If we use one species of symbols, it is called pure notation. If we use more than one species it is called mixed notations. There was a time when pure notation was preferred than mixed notation. But in the time of interdisciplinary research and development of complex subjects, the mixed notation is preferred and used by most of the classification schemes.

Classification schemes whether DC, Bliss, LC, UDC and CC have adopted mixed notation in their latest revised editions. Every scheme has used more than one species though few classification schemes have enumerative structure. Notations should be such that may be shorter and ensure coextensiveness, which could differentiate between the facet of any class either by an apportionment of symbols or by facet indicators; its needs to be able to indicate phase changes and to show which phase is being used. All this points to at least three or four species of notations. Notation should be flexible.

18.6 Notation Flexibility

Flexibility can be explained by an example: Suppose book cases were lettered A-Z and the shelves within each were numbered 1-30, then a book with the symbol G 25 on its back would belong to 25th shelf of case G. More books shelf number and case number may be altered as per requirement. Knowledge is ever-growing and it is difficult to enumerate existing subjects, while future subjects are beyond our reach. We leave gap in our numbers using intelligent anticipation as to future requirements. This was done by Brown and Dewey in their classification. A partial solution can be found in the use of numbers read as a decimal fraction. Decimal implies division in ten parts but only 9 sub-divisions are accommodated (DC).

65	Building
651	Estimating
653	Masonry
655	Plastering
657	Plumbering

The decimal notation proves to be hospitable to increase in chain, but not in array. Hence notation can meet expansion due to new coordinate as well as new subordinate: one which will offer hospitability in array as well as chain.

Ranganathan developed it by using a colon to separate one facet from another. A notation which thus takes cognizance of change of characteristics, and separates the various facets of subjects is called a faceted notation. – L4:42. A faceted notation allows us to mechanise the order of the facets to show where we change the characteristic used for division.

18.7 Mnemonics

Knowledge is consistently increasing and that the new subjects are always arising. There are few concepts which repeat in each schedule. Similar notation of similar concept should be constructed in each schedule as to memorise or revise them easily. For example problems, disease, etc. are effected in many schedules in CC and DC. There are provisions of common notations, i.e. common isolates, language and time isolates and also more in schedules also. The mnemonics given in schedule as list, division are known as scheduled mnemonics.

18.8 Facet Formula

Ranganathan used facet formula. He used five facets in colon classification — personality, matter, energy, space and time. The only independent variable is personality, which determines the specific subject deduced from matrix. This effort of Ranganathan is appreciated that classifying will consist of breaking down the specific subject to be classified into terms of formula, and the assigning a class number must consist of fitting together according to the rules of the scheme the symbols for each specified part of the formula. DDC preferred to consult index while Sayers and Ranganathan both warm against using the index.

The fundamental concepts are a generalized statement of the parts of every specific subject and are the basis of Ranganathan's facet formula.

While consulting the classification schemes and constructing the number, the following stages should be followed:

1. Write out the exact specific subject of the book.

2. Break down all composite terms used by the author in describing the nature of his subject.

3. Decide whether it is a single or multi phased subject.

4. If multiphases, mark-off each phase and determine the nature of relationship between the phases.

5. From the nature of the relation, determine which is the primary phase.

6. Taking the primary phase first, determine the class to which subject belongs.

7. Write down the facet formula.

8. Substitute for the general terms of the formula the appropriate terms of the specific subject, putting the word 'diffuse' where a facet is not specified in the subject.

9. Turn up the class in the schedule and write down the digit which corresponds to it.

10. Look in the schedule for that group of division of class which corresponds with the first facet specified in the formula and add the appropriate digit to the class number.

11. Complete the class number by assembling the phases using the symbols with the help of supplement tables.

19

Specific Features of Seventh Edition (1971) of CC

Library classification is a field of universe of subjects. It arranges subjects:

1. In a linear sequence helpful to the majority of readers.
2. To mechanise the arrangement by representing each subject by a unique ordinal number.

Since 1950, a dynamic theory of classification is being developed as a basis for scheme of classification. Theory is the separation of idea plane and in the Notational plains. Idea plane is paramount. The versatility of the national plane should be continuously increased to enable it to implement the findings of the idea plane in respect of the sequence of subjects—past, present and future, 7th Edition:

1. Main subjects are increased to 105.
   (a) 34 involve correction work,
   (b) 13 of these do not involve change of plane,
   (c) but 21 do. These are new subjects and do not have much literacy warrant.
2. The concept of "Matter-property" Isolates have been developed.
3. Many of the isolates forcedly deemed to be manifestations of energy in the past have now been brought into this new category. This only involve

change of indicator digit ":" Colon into ";" (semicolon), but no change of place.

4. New indicator digits have been introduced for authorizing isolates and for phase relation, without involving change of place.

5. The insertion of indicator digit "," (comma) is made obligatory even in the level of first personality.

6. The capacity of an array in the notational plane has been increased considerably.

7. Any amount of interpolation at any point in an array has been made possible with the use of emptying digits.

8. Annexure 1 gives the new and the old facet formula for the diverse basic subjects:

1. Main Subjects and Partial Comprehensions

11 *Schedule of Main Subjects and Partial Comprehensions:*

The Table following the abbreviations list gives a schedule of Main Subjects and Partial Comprehensions. It gives also successively the Class Number according to Edition 7 (1971), Class Number according to Edition 6 (1960), and the nature of the changes, in respect of each subject as between Edition 6 and Edition 7:

19.1 Abbreviations

FM   = Fused Main Subject.

ND   = New Distilled Main Subject.

NM   = New Main Subject other than Distilled and Fused Ones.

NM/CS = New Main Subject formerly a Canonical Subject or a Compound Subject or a System Basic Subject.

NP   = New Partial Comprehensions.

OD/CP = Old Distilled Main Subject with Change of Class Number and Place.

OM/CN = Old Main Subject with Change of Class Number but No Change of Place.

OM/NC = Old Main Subject with No Change of Class Number of Place.

OP/CN = Old Partial Comprehension with Change of Class Number but No Change of Place.

OP/NC = Old Partial Comprehension with No Change of Class Number.

Note: 1. The name of each Partial Comprehension is in Italics.

2. The name of each Fused Main Subject is in Block Face.

3. The name of each of the other New Main Subjects, including New Distilled Main Subject, is in capitals and small capitals.

S. No.	Subject	Ed 7 1971	Ed 6 1960	OM NC	OM CN	NM CS	OD CP	ND	FM	NM	OP NC	OP CN	NP
1.	*Generalia*	z	Z	Yes									
2.	Universe of Subject: Structure & Develop.	1	1	Yes									
3.	Library Science	2	2	Yes									
4.	Book Science	3	3	Yes									
5.	Reading Method	3V								Yes			
6.	Notes Taking	3X								Yes			
7.	Journalism	4	4	Yes									
8.	Exhibition Technique	5						Yes					
9.	Museology	6						Yes					
10.	Systemology	7						Yes					
11.	Management Science	8	(X)				Yes						
12.	Career	9b						Yes					
13.	Metrology	9c						Yes					
14.	Standardisation	9d						Yes					
15.	Research Methodology	9f						Yes					
16.	Evaluation Technique	9g	(:g)				Yes						
17.	Conference Technique	9p	(p)				Yes						
18.	Seminar Technique	9s						Yes					
19.	Commission Technique	9t						Yes					
20.	Communication	9p	(P)				Yes						
21.	Symbolism	9Q						Yes					
22.	Natural and Social Sciences	9ZZ												Yes

No.	Subject	Code 1	Code 2								
23.	Natural Science	A	A						Yes		
24.	Mathematical Science	AZ	β							Yes	Yes
25.	Mathematics	B	B	Yes							
26.	Statistical Analysis	BT	B28	Yes	Yes						
27.	Operational Research	BTT						Yes			
28.	Cybernetics	BV				Yes					
29.	Astronomy and Astrophysics	BWZ									Yes
30.	Astronomy	BX	B9		Yes						
31.	Astrophysics	BXT	B9:6				Yes				
32.	Physical Science	BZ	T							Yes	
33.	Physics	C	C	Yes							
34.	Space Physics	CV						Yes			
35.	Engineering and Technology	CZ									Yes
36.	Engineering	D	D	Yes							
37.	Draughtmanship	DV		Yes							
38.	Chemical Science	DZ						Yes		Yes	
39.	Chemistry	E	E	Yes							Yes
40.	Chemical Engineering	DYE	D: (E)	Yes			Yes				
41.	Technology	F	F	Yes							
42.	Biological Science	FZ		Yes							
43.	Biology	G	G								Yes
44.	Microbiology	GT	G91	Yes	Yes						

Contd...

S. No.	Subject	Ed 7 1971	Ed 6 1960	OM NC	OM CN	NM CS	OD CP	ND	FM	NM	OP NC	OP CN	NP
45.	Molecular Biology	GUA											Yes
46.	Biomechanics	GUB	G:(B7)						Yes				
47.	Biophysics	GUC	G:(C)						Yes				
48.	Biochemistry	GUE	E9G						Yes				Yes
49.	Geological Science	GZ											
50.	Geology	H	H	Yes									
51.	Geodesy	HUB							Yes				
52.	Geophysics	HV	H: (C)						Yes				
53.	Geochemistry	HVT	H : (E)						Yes				
54.	Mining	HX	HZ		Yes								
55.	Plant Science	HZ											Yes
56.	Botany	I	I	Yes									Yes
57.	Agriculture Forestry and Animal Husbandry	IZ											
58.	Agriculture	J	J	Yes									
59.	Forestry	JX	JB			Yes							
60.	Animal Science	JZ		Yes									Yes
61.	Zoology	K	K		Yes								
62.	Animal Husbandry	KX	KZ										Yes
63.	Medical Science	KZ											
64.	Medicine	L	L	Yes									
65.	Medical Technology	LT								Yes			
66.	Public Health	LU5	L:5			Yes							

No.	Subject								
67.	Hospital and Sanitorium	LU5Z							Yes
68.	Hospital	LU5	L:14	Yes	Yes				
69.	Sanitorium	LU7	L:15	Yes	Yes				
70.	Pharmacognosy	LX	LZ		Yes	Yes			
71.	Nursing	LYI	L:4:1			Yes			
72.	Medical Jurisprudence	LYX	L:(Z)						
73.	Useful Arts	M	M	Yes				Yes	
74.	Humanities and Social Science	MZ	μ	Yes				Yes	
75.	Humanities	MZZ	ν						
76.	Mysticism and Spiritual Experience	Δ	Δ	Yes			Yes		
77.	Fine Arts	N	N	Yes			Yes		
78.	Language & Literature	NZ	NZ	Yes			Yes		
79.	Literature	O	O	Yes					
80.	Linguistics	P	P	Yes					
81.	Calligraphy	PU1	P (1)		Yes				
82.	Typewriting	PU6	P (6)		Yes				
83.	Shorthand	PU7	P (3)		Yes				
84.	Religion and Philosophy	PZ							Yes
85.	Religion and Ethics	PZZ							Yes
86.	Religion	Q	Q	Yes					
87.	Philosophy and Psychology	QZ							Yes

Contd...

S. No.	Subject	Ed 7 1971	Ed 6 1960	OM NC	OM CN	NM CS	OD CP	ND	FM	NM	OP NC	OP CN	NP
88.	Philosophy	R	R	Yes									
89.	Psychology and Education	RZ											Yes
90.	Psychology	S	S	Yes									
91.	Applied Psychology	SX	Σ							Yes			
92.	Social Science	SZ											Yes	
93.	Education	T	T	Yes									
94.	Geography and History	TZ											Yes
95.	Geography	U	U	Yes									
96.	History, Political Science and Economics	UZ												Yes
97.	History	V	V	Yes									
98.	Historical Source (as a Pure Discipline)	VT						Yes					
99.	Political Science	W	W	Yes									
100.	Geopolitics	WV	WOgU						Yes				
101.	Economics	X	X	Yes									
102.	Economics of Industry	XX	X8 (A)			Yes							
103.	Sociology	Y	Y	Yes	Yes								
104.	Social work	YX	YZ	Yes									
105.	Law	Z	Z	Yes									
		105	46	31	4	12	4	12	12	7	1	5	18

Note: In Ed 6 "(r) Administration Report Technique was enumerated among the Main Subjects. Therefore, the number of Main Subjects in Ed 6, as found in the Schedule of Main Subjects, is 47 instead of 46 as shown in the above Table. In Ed 7, this subject has become a Compound Subject going with the Main Subject "3 Book Science".

12. *Census of Main Subjects and Partial Comprehensions*

Number of Main Subjects and Partial Comprehensions in Ed 7	105
-do- in Ed 6	46
Number of New Main Subjects and New Partial Comprehensions in Ed 7	59

121. *Census of New Main Subjects and New Partial Comprehensions*

Number of New Main Subjects and New Partial Comprehensions	59
These 59 are made of the following:	
Number of subjects involving no correction work	
New Distilled Main Subjects	12
Other New Main Subjects	8
New Partial Comprehensions	18
Total	38
Number of New Main Subjects converted from the Old Non-Main Subjects involving correction work	21
	59

122. *Census of New Main Subjects Involving Correction Work*

Number of subjects involving correction work	21
These 21 are made of the following:	
Number of subjects involving correction work but no change of place	4

Number of subjects involving correction
work as well as change of place   17
                                                    21

123. *Census of New Main Subjects Involving Change of Place*

Number of New Main Subjects involving
correction work as well as change of place.   17

These 17 are made of the following:
Fused Main Subjects   10
New Main subjects formerly Canonical or
Compound Subjects   7
                                                   17

13. *Census of Old Main Subjects and Old Partial Comprehensions*

Number of Old Main Subjects and Old Partial
Comprehensions of Ed 6 involving
correction work   13

These 13 are made of the following:
Number of subjects involving correction
work but no change of place   9
Number of subjects involving
correction work as well as change
of place   4
                                                   13

131. *Census of Old Main Subjects and Partial Comprehensions Involving Correction Work, But No Change of Place*

Number of subjects involving correction work
but no change of place   9

These 9 are made of the following:
Old Main Subjects other than Old Distilled
Main Subjects ·   4
Old Partial Comprehensions   5
                                                    9

14. *Overall Census*

Number of Main Subjects and Partial Comprehensions in Ed 7	105
These 105 are made of the following:	
Number of subjects not involving correction work	71
Number of subjects involving correction work	34
	105

141. *Census of Subjects Involving Correction*

Number of Subjects involving correction work	34
These 34 are made of the following:	
Number of subjects not involving correction work but no change of place	13
Number of subjects involving correction work as well as change of place	21
	34

142. *Census of Main Subjects and Partial Comprehensions*

Involving Correction Work but no Change of Place Number of Main Subjects and Partial Comprehensions involving correction work but no change of place	13
These 13 are made of the following:	
Partial Comprehensions	5
Main Subjects	8
	13

143. *Census of Main Subjects Involving Correction as well as Change of Place*

Number of Main Subjects involving correction work as well as change of place	21
These 21 are made of the following:	
Distilled Main Subjects	4
Fused Main Subjects	10
Other Main Subjects	7
	21

15. No Need for Correction Work

Out of the 105 Main Subjects and Partial Comprehensions in Ed 7, 71 do not require any correction work. Twenty-five of them are new subjects attracting literary warrant only recently. Thus these do not add any load to correction work.

16. No Urgency in Correction Work

Out of the 105 Main Subjects and Partial Comprehensions in Ed 7, 13 Main Subjects involve correction work but no change of place. These are the following:

1. **Five Partial Comprehensions**: Mathematical Sciences, Physical Sciences, Humanities, Literature and Language, and Social Science.

2. **Eight Main Subjects**: Mining, Forestry, Animal Husbandry, Pharmacognosy, Calligraphy, Typewriting, Shorthand and Social Work.

In each of these subjects, the books having old Class Numbers and those with new Class Numbers will come together in one and the same place, but in two distinct groups. This will cause no serious difficulty to the reader or to the library staff. Therefore, there is no urgency for correction work in these 13 subjects. It can be done slowly at leisure.

161. The number of books and periodicals in any one of the 5 Partial Comprehensions mentioned in Sec 16 will be very small.

162. In Service Libraries, other than the Specialist Libraries concerned, the number of books and periodicals in any one of the 8 Main Subjects mentioned in Sec 16 will not be large.

17. Correction Work Involved in Distilled Main Subjects

The following 4 Distilled Main Subjects involve correction work as well as change of place: Evaluation Technique; Conference Technique; Communication and Management. This should be done immediately.

171. Among the 4 Distilled Main Subjects mentioned in Sec 17, the first three subjects are of recent origin. They are not likely to have more than a dozen books in any library. But the pure discipline of Management has been attracting literary

warrant for about two decades. Even then, in a service library, other than a Specialist Library in "Management", there may not be more than fifty books on the subject. Thus, the correction work involved is relatively small.

18. *Correction Work Involved in Fused Main Subjects*

Fused Main Subjects appear for the first time in Ed 7. Till now, they were treated as Compound Subjects. Therefore, they involve correction work as well as change of place. They are only 10 in number, and they are the following:

Astrophysics	Biophysics	Geochemistry
Chemistry	Biochemistry	Medical Jurisprudence
Engineering	Geodesy	Geopolitics
Biomechanics	Geophysics	

181. Among the 10 subjects mentioned in Sec 18, the 6 Subjects Biomechanics, Biophysics, Geodesy, Geochemistry, and Geopolitics, and Historical Source may not have much literary warrant.

182. But Biochemistry and Geophysics will have much of literary warrant. Here, the term 'Geophysics' denotes a Main Subject with the following as Canonical Basic Subjects:

Geoelectricity	Oceanology
Geomagnetism	Meteorology
Internal Geodynamics	Aerology (Upper Air Physics)
Hydrogeology	

The correction work involved in these seven Fused Main Subjects will be appreciably large.

191. *Correction Work in Other New Main Subjects*

The following 9 subjects are deemed to be new Main Subjects in Ed 7: Statistical Analysis, Astronomy, Astrophysics, Microbiology, Public Health, Hospital, Sanitorium, Nursing, and Economics of Industries. Till now, the first two were listed as Canonical Divisions of Mathematics. The last seven were treated as Compound Subjects. Therefore, they involve correction work as well as change of place. These subjects have had considerable literary warrant for several years. Therefore, the correction work involved will be considerable. In respect of "BT

Statistical Analysis", it must be remembered, while collecting books for correction, that this subject can appear as phase 2 of Complex Subjects. These can be located with the aid of the entries under the heading "Statistical Analysis" in the alphabetical part of the catalogue.

19.2 Basic Subjects

Ed 7 has increased the number of Basic Subjects. This has been done in several ways.

21. Some Old Main subjects such as "3 Book Science" and some new Main Subjects such as "9 Research Technique" have been divided into Canonical Divisions. In these cases Literary warrant is developing now.

22. In some subjects, such as "D Engineering" "F Technology", "U Geography", and "X Economics". Round 1, Level 1'(P) Isolates have been treated as Canonical Divisions. Experience has shown this to be helpful. For, the Compound Subjects going with them require their own respective different schedule of Special Isolates. In these cases, there will be no need for correction work.

23. In "X Economics", some of the (E) Isolates have been changed into Canonical Divisions. However, their literary warrant is small. Therefore, the correction work needed will be small.

24. A new kind of formation of subjects, namely Subject Bundles (See Sec 053, Category 94) — has been added as Canonical Division of "A Natural Science". Perhaps a similar thing may become necessary in respect of some other Partial Comprehensions also. These Subject Bundles are gaining literary warrant, only just now. Therefore, there will be no need for much correction work.

25. Systems have been changed into Basic Subjects.

26. Specials have been changed into Basic Subjects.

27. A device—"Environmental Device"—has been provided to indicate environmented treatment of a Main Subject, as a kind of Specials. Such a treatment is included in the Schedule of Specials Basic Subjects.

28. Compound Basic Subjects—using the System part Specials part, and Canonical Division part as its components — have been provided for (See Sec 051, Category 914). There is literary warrant for this. The indicator Digit for each of the second and later components of a compound Basic subject is "-" (hyphen). Originally, these components were treated as isolates in different Levels in Round 1; therefore had "," (comma) as the Indicator Digit. Hence, these cases require correction. But literary warrant has been negligibly small in these cases. Therefore, the correction work needed will also be negligibly small.

291. Compound Isolate Facets have been occasionally used in the earlier editions of Colon Classification (See Sec 051, Category 92). They have to be used very much in depth classification—particularly, for Production Engineering and Production Technology. The need for Compound (P) Isolate Facets with even ten or more components has arisen in many subjects. Apart from this, even at book-level Compound (S) Isolate Facets are now becoming necessary (11). For this purpose, the divisions shown under "1 World" in the Schedule of Space Isolates in Ed 6, made of non-territorial divisions of the world, had to be changed slightly. The digit "0" (Zero) is to be prefixed to the Subject Device division number. Further, the digit "Z" is to be prefixed to the number of the Imperial Country in the number for an Empire. Each of the non-territorial divisions should be regarded as second or later component of (S) Isolate Facet with "1 World" as the first component. The digit "-" (hyphen) should be used as the indicator Digit for the number representing each of the non-territorial divisions. The kind of Divisions can also be used to form Compound Space Isolates with a continent, a country, a constituent State, or any other territorial division, and of any Population Cluster as the Host Isolate.

Examples:

1-0 (P,111)	English speaking countries
1-A	Near-Sovereign formation
1-N4	United Nations area

1-Z56	British empire
1-Z56-0 (P,111)	English speaking countries in the British empire
4	Asia
4-97	Pacific countries of Asia
4-97-0 (J,381)	Rice belt of the Pacific countries of Asia
44	India
44-9J	Western region
44-Z4435	Maharashtra empire
44-Z45	Moghul India
44-Z56	British India
4411	Tamil Nadu
4411-0 (J,781)	Cotton belt of Tamil Nadu
4411-952	Arabian front of Tamil Nadu
44112	Chingleput District.

If Compound Isolates have not been used for the non-territorial divisions—that is to say, if the indicator Digit "-"(hyphen) had not been used before the non-territorial components—the sequence in the above illustrative schedule would become quite unhelpful. For example "44 India" would have come before the non-territorial divisions of "4 Asia" such as "497 Pacific countries of Asia". A similar thing would have happened in the case of India. To gain a richer experience of this phenomenon, the (S) Isolates in the above illustrative schedule may be re-arranged, dropping the digit "-" (hyphen), "0" (Zero), and "Z", wherever they occur.

292. An advance account of what is said in Sec 25 to 28 has already been published (20).

293. A tentative advance list of Basic Subjects including Main Subjects and Partial Comprehensions has already been published (22). It will form Chapter EQ OF CC, Ed 7.

19.3 Common Isolates

Anteriorising Common Isolates

The indicator Digit— "—(Double inverted comma) is used to indicate an "Anteriorising Isolate". As stated in Sec 0863, this releases the Roman small letters for use in the formation of arrays in the same manner as the Indo-Arabic numerals and the Roman capital letters. Further, while working on the design of Electronic Doc- Finder, it was found convenient of all Roman small letters (18, 36).

32 *Examples*

1 Bibliography of Mathematics will be represented by B "a" and not by Ba.

2 Encyclopaedia of Mathematics will be represented by B "k" and not by Bk.

3 Journal of the Indian Mathematical Society will be represented by B "m44, N", and not by Bm44, N.

The insertion of __"__(double inverted comma) could be made easily without rewriting the whole Class Number.

33. *No Urgency for Correction*

The majority of corrections in this category will be concerned with "m Periodicals", "n Serials", "r Periodical Reports", and "x Collected works". The number of cases of other Anteriorising Common Isolates will not be large. Moreover, in the former cases, the uncorrected and the corrected numbers can be arranged together without any difficulty. Therefore, the correction of the old volumes need not be done immediately. It can be spread over a long term—even years.

34. *Common Fundamental Category Isolates*

Ed. 7 includes common Fundamental Category Isolates— For (E), (MP), and (P). As they are mostly new, these will not require any correction work. An advance list of such Common Isolate had already been published (30, 50, 57).

4. *Phase Relation*

The new Indicator Digit "&" (ampersand) is used in the place of the old Indicator Digit "0" (Zero) for Phase Relation.

41. As stated in Sec 0863, this releases the digit "0"(Zero) for use in an array as in the case of the other Indo-Arabic numerals and the Roman capital letters (17, 37).

42. The number of Phased Class Numbers is not large.

Therefore, the correction work in this case will not be much. The digit "0"(Zero) can be easily changed into the digit "&" (ampersand) without rewriting the whole Class Number.

5. *Change of some [E] Isolates into [MP] Isolates:*

51. Since 1967, the schedule of (E), (E) cum (2P), (2E), and (2E) cum (3P) Isolates are being systematically examined as part of the preparation of Ed 7.

52. The sub-divisions 54 onwards give a brief outline of the changes of this kind already marked out for inclusion in Ed 7.

53. *No Urgency in Correction Work*

As a result of the changes of this kind the Indicator Digit should be changed from ":" (colon) to ";" (semicolon). These changes will require a considerable amount of correction work, in most cases. However, the new books and the corrected old ones on the one hand, and the uncorrected old books on the other, will come together in the same place, but in two distinct groups. This will cause no serious difficulty to the reader or to the library staff. Therefore, there is no urgency for correction work in these cases. It can be done slowly at leisure. But books that do not satisfy this condition should be corrected very early; and they will not be many.

54. *Change of (E) Isolates into (MP) Isolates*

The following Table gives the changeover in the schedules for different Basic Subjects, from under the heading (E) Isolates to under the heading (MP) Isolates:

	Basic Subject	Cases of Changeover
B23	Theory of Equation	All (E) Isolates
C7	Magnetism	All (E) Isolates
J	Agriculture	All (E) Isolates
JX	Forestry	All (E) Isolates
KX	Animal Husbandry	The Isolates "2 Morphology", "3 Physiology", "4 Disease" and "5 Hygiene" only.

541. *Examples of the Change*

	Class Number	
Subject	Ed 7 (New)	Ed 6 (Old)
Formal Solution of Cubic Equation	B,233;5	B233:5
Virus Disease of Rice Plant	J,381;423	J381:423
Morphology of the Cow	KX,311;2	KX311:2

55. *Change of (E) cum (2P) Isolates into (MP) Isolates*

The following Table gives the changeover in the schedules for different Basic Subjects, from under the heading (E) cum (2P) Isolates to under the heading (MP) Isolates:

	Basic Subject	Cases of Changeover
2	Library Science	All (E) cum (2P) Isolates other than "97 Documentation"
B13	Theory of Integers	All (E) cum (2P) Isolates
B15	Algebraic Number and Ideal Number	All (E) cum (2P) Isolates
B16	Complex and Hyper-Complex Numbers	All (E) cum (2P) Isolates
B25	Higher Algebra	All (E) cum (2P) Isolates
B33	Differential and Intergral Equation	All (E) cum (2P) Isolates
B37	Real Variable	All (E) cum (2P) Isolates
B38	Complex Variable	All (E) cum (2P) Isolates
B7	Mechanics	All (E) cum (2P) Isolates
C2	Properties of Matter	All (P2) Isolates

Contd...

	Basic Subject	Cases of Changeover
C3	Sound	All (E) cum (2P) Isolates
C4	Heat	All (E) cum (2P) Isolates
C5	Radiation	All (E) cum (2P) Isolates
C6	Electricity	All (E) cum (2P) Isolates
C9B3	Nuclear Physics	All (E) cum (2P) Isolates
E	Chemistry	All (E) cum (2P) Isolates other than "3 Analytical chemistry" "4 Synthesis", "5 Extraction", and "8 Manipulation" and their divisions
F	Technology	All (E) cum (2P) Isolates except "Manipulation" divisions
G	Biology	All (E) cum (2P) Isolates other than "8 Manipulation"
I	Botany	Same as that for the Main subject "G Biology"
K	Zoology	Same as that for the Main subject "G Biology" and in addition the following: "591 Relation to Young Ones" and "595 Courting"
L	Medicine	All (E) cum (2P) Isolates other than "5 Public Health and Hygiene and their divisions (*Note:* In Ed 7 "5" represents Hygiene instead of "57")
Δ	Spiritual Experience and Mysticism	All (E) cum (2P) Isolates
P	Linguistics	All (E) cum (2P) Isolates
Q	Religion	All (E) cum (2P) Isolates
S	Psychology	All (E) cum (2P) Isolates
T	Education	All (E) cum (2P) Isolates
V	History	All (E) cum (2P) Isolates
X	Economics	(Under consideration)
W	Political Science	Same as that for the Main Subject "V History"
Y	Sociology	All (E) cum (2P) Isolates

551. *Examples of the Change*

S.N.	Subject	Class Number	
		Ed 7 (New)	Ed 6 (Old)
1.	Library Classification	2; 51	2:51
2.	Representation of a function of Real Variable as Infinite Series	B37; 26	B37:26
3.	Kinetics of Rigid Body	B7,13; 32	B713:32
4.	Diffraction of X-rays	C5,3; 55	C53:55
5.	Chemical Kinetics *Note:* Subjects at SN 6 to 11 Go with the Main Subject "Medicine"		
6.	Tuberculosis	L; 421	L:421
7.	Tuberculosis of the Lungs	L,45; 421	L45:421
8.	Tuberculosis of the Lungs of A Child	L9C,45; 421	L9C,45; 421
9.	Tuberculosis of the Lungs According to Ayurveda	LB,45; 421	LB,45; 421
10.	Child Medicine in Ayurveda	LB-9C	LB,9C
11.	Tuberculosis of the Lungs of a child according to Ayurveda	LB-9C,45; 421	LB,9C,45: 421
12.	(Psychology of) Anger	S;524	S:524
13.	Anger of the Old	S,38; 524	S38:524
14.	Anger of a Refugee	S9B; 524	
15.	Psychoanalysis of Anger	SM9; 524	SM9:524
16.	Psychoanalysis of Refugee	SM9-9B	
17.	Psychoanalysis of the Anger of the Refugee	SM9-9B; 524	
18.	Functions of the President of USA, brought upto 1950's	V73,1; 3 'N5	V73,1:3 'N5
19.	Function of the head of a Democratic State	W,6,1; 3	W6,1:3
20.	Marriage Ceremony in Christian Community	Y,73(Q6); 317	Y73(Q6):317

56. *Change of (2E) Isolate into (E) Isolate*

The following Table gives the changeover in the schedule for a Basic Subject, to under the heading (E) from under the heading (2E) in respect of those isolates in (E), and (E) cum (2P) changed into isolates in (MP):

Basic Subject	Cases of Changeover
J Agriculture	All (2E) Isolates

561. *Examples of the Change:*

SN	Subject	Class Number	
		Ed 7 (New)	Ed 6 (Old)
1.	Sowing the seeds in paddy cultivation	J,381; 38:3	J381:38:3
2.	Prevention of the virus disease of the rice plant	J,381; 423:5	J381:423:5
3.	Curing the rice after harvest	J,381; 78:6	J381:78:6

Here, the term 'Harvest' gives trouble in the Verbal Plane. We will be replacing it by a suitable term very soon.

57. *Breaking of (2E) Cum (3P) Isolates into (E) Isolates and (2P) Isolates*

The following table gives the changeover in the schedules for a Basic Subject, to under the heading (E), (2P) from under the heading (2E) cum (3P) in respect of those isolates in (E), and (E) cum (2P) changed to (MP) isolates:

Basic Subject	Cases of Changeover
L Medicine	All (2E) cum (3P) Isolates

571. *Examples of the Change:*

SN	Subject	Class Number	
		Ed 7 (New)	Ed 6 (Old)
	X-Ray therapy of the tuberculosis of the Lungs	L,45; 421:6,253	L45:421:6253

19.4 Change in Facet Structure

581. A facet formula is in a sense meaningless; it is indeed an anachronism.

582. However it may be of help for the beginners and for those that have been accustomed to its use in Ed 6, if the facet structure for the commonly occurring Compound subjects is given.

583. The Table in Annexure 2 gives such facet structures. Col. 1 gives the Host Basic subject along with its Class Number. Col. 2 gives the facet Structure of Compound subjects to be used in Ed 7. Col. 3 gives the corresponding facet structure used in Ed. 6. In the copy of the Colon Classification used by the classifier, changing the facet structure accordingly will be helpful till Ed 7 is acquired.

6. Personality Facet: Level 1

61. In many cases of the depth classification of articles, the number of digit in the host non-Main Basic class number and in the Round 1, Level 1 of [P] taken together exceeds the maximum limit six, set by comfort of the physiology of the eyes and of the psychology of memory (53). So it was in respect of [E] cum [2P] numbers. To avoid this, the indicator Digit ",", (comma) should be inserted before Level 1 of (P) facet in any Round in any subject, whether the Host subject is a Main subject or a non-Main Basic subject. For this purpose the Rules 05502 and 05503 in part 1 of Colon Classification, Ed 6 (1960) and the corresponding rules in earlier editions are deleted (See Sec 086).

62. This change requires correction work in the case of many Compound subjects. This does not mean, however, "all subjects". The volumes of periodical publications and the books, belonging to simple subjects without any (P) isolates, facets will not need this correction; and most of the periodical publications are of this kind. These form a considerable part of the collection in a library.

63. Further, this correction need not be done immediately. It can be spread over some time. In the case of books, the new

ones and the corrected old ones will come before the old uncorrected books. This will be a temporary advantage. For, the most used books will come earlier than the less used ones.

7. Personality Facet: Two or More Levels

71. All the special facets in any Compound subject going with the Main subject "O Literature" or with "Z" Law are [P]; and these belong to different Levels. Further, it is conjectured that a predetermined facet structure can be used for the Compound subjects going with each of these two Main Subjects. In most cases each Level is possible only if its Immediate Earlier Level occurs. If however, it happens that a facet occurs without its prescribed Immediate Earlier Level preceding it, the digit "0" (Zero) should be prefixed to the Isolate Number in the Level actually occurring.

Examples:

> 0,111,1   English Poetry; but
>
> 0,01   Poetry in general

As a result, the second subject will come earlier than the first. This will satisfy the Canon of Decreasing Extension (32).

72. It is conjectured that the first two Levels of round 1 [P] can be pre-determined for the Compound subjects going with the Main subject "V History" —the Country Facet, and the facet made of the Organ of the Government of the Country. The latter cannot occur without the first preceding it. It is conjectured that similar is the case with the Basic subjects "B25 Algebraic Transformation" and "B33 Differential and Integral Equations."

73. It is conjectured that the first two Levels of round [P] can be predetermined for the Compound subjects going with the following Basic subjects:

HX	Mining	D	Spiritual Experience and Mysticism
I	Botany	R3	Metaphysics
K	Zoology	R4	Ethics
LX5	Pharmacopoeia	W	Political Science

In these cases, the prescribed Level 2 can occur without Level 1.

If so, the digit "0" (Zero) should be prefixed to the Isolate Number in Level 2 of [P].

Example:

> I,015   Leaf of a plant; but
>
> I,5,15   Leaf of a flowering plant.

74. In the case of the Basic subjects with "N" Fine arts as the host Main subject, what was prescribed in Ed 6 as [P] and [P2] for jointly representing style in Ed 6 have now been changed into a System which is individualised successively by (GD) and (CD). The result is a System Basic subject. If the (CD) number occurs in the system number, it must be preceded by the indicator Digit "-" (hyphen).

Example:

> In the place of
>
> ND44,C Buddhist Sculpture
>
> we now have
>
> ND(44-C) Buddhist Sculpture.

The old style number is now treated as system number. In this case, the system number begins with an Indo-Arabic numeral, whereas in other cases it begins with a Roman capital letter. A system number should come last in the array of the non-main part of a Basic subject. It is to secure this that the system number is enclosed in circular brackets in this case. Incidentally, this packet Notation makes the system number as if it were a single digit. The resulting system number (44-C), for example, is a Compound System Number. After this change is made [P3] and [P4]. Therefore, they should be re-named [P1] and [P2]—that is Round 1, Levels 1 and 2 of [P]. These new predetermined Levels 1 and 2 of [P] may be dealt with on the analogy given in Sec 73.

75. In the case of the Main subject "P Linguistics", what was prescribed as [P] and [P2] in Ed 6 have now been changed into components of a Compound Isolate.

Example:

In the place of

P111,J,9D56175   Yorkshire Dialect of Modern English

we now have

P,111-J-9D56175   Yorkshire Dialect of Modern English.

The resulting Isolate is a Compound Isolate. After this change is made, [P3] will be the only surviving predetermined Level in Round 1 of [P]. Therefore, it should be re-named [P]— that is, Round 1 Level 1 of [P].

8. Correction Work

81. *Incidence of Correction Work*

All books accessioned after a definite epoch, say 1 October 1969 should be classified according to Ed 7. The Class Number of the older books should be corrected, wherever warranted.

The incidence of correction work is not equally heavy in all subjects. The difference in the heaviness of the correction work to be done has been indicated in earlier sections.

Again the urgency of the correction work is not the same in all subjects. The difference in the urgency of correction work to be done has indicated in earlier sections.

82. *Difference between Local Service Library and State or National Central Library*

The term 'Local Service Library' includes public library, school library, college library, university library, and specialist library.

The number of old books whose class numbers are to be corrected will be much less in a Local Service Library or in the Service Collection of a State or National Central Library than in the Dormitory Collection of either of these. For, in a Local Service Library worn-out books and books outmoded in thought or in method of presentation would have been weeded out from time to time. The average number of volumes may not exceed— indeed, should not exceed—about 50,000 in a Local Service Library. In a City or a District Central Library, the live-collection may exceed 50,000 volumes. But most of them will be copies of one and the same book intended for use in the Branch Libraries.

In a University Library, the upper limit to the number of volumes may have to go upto 3,00,000. If the number of volumes exceeds any prescribed upper limit, the outmoded books should be transferred to the Dormitory Collection of the State Central Library (43). Further, a large number of the volumes held in a University Library will be made of long sets of periodical publications and collected works. As stated in sector there is no urgency for correction work in these cases.

The correction work in a Dormitory collection in a State or National Central Library may be left to the Method of Osmosis (). Most of this collection can be left to remain with the old class numbers. To pick out any volume of this collection, occasionally needed, all that the library will have to do is to maintain a conversion table showing in parallel columns the new class number and the equivalent old class numbers.

Facet Structure

	Basic Subject	Facet Formula	
		Ed 7 (1971)	Ed 6 (1960)
2	Library Science	2, [P]; [MP]	2[P];[M]:[E][2P]
B13	Theory of Integers	B13,[P],[P2];[MP]	B13[P],[P2]:[E][2P]
B15	Algebraic Number & Ideal	B15,[P],[P2];[MP]	B15[P],[P2]:[E][2P]
B16	Complex and Hyper-Complex Number	B16,[P],[P2];[MP]	B16[P],[P2]:[E][2P]
B23	Theory of Equation	B23,[P];[MP]	B23[P]:[E]
B25	Higher Algebra	B25,[P],[P2];[MP]	B25[P],[P2]:[E][2P]
B33	Differential and Integral Equations	B33,[P],[P2],[P3];[MP]	B33[P],[P2],[P3]:[E][2P]
B37	Real Variable	B37,[P];[MP]	B37[P]:[E] [2P]
B38	Complex Variable	B38,[P];[MP]	B38[P]:[E] [2P]
B6	Geometry	B6,[P];[MP]	B6[P]:[E] [2P]
B7	Mechanics	B7,[P];[MP]	B7[P]:[E][2P]
BV	Astronomy	BV,[P];[MP]	B9[P]:[E][2P]
C2	Properties of Matter	C2,[P];[MP]	C2[P1]:[P2]
C3	Sound	C3,[P];[MP]	C3[P]:[E][2P]
C4	Heat	C4,[P];[MP]	C4[P]:[E][2P]
C5	Radiation	C5,[P];[MP]	C5[P]:[E][2P]
C6	Electricity	C6,[P];[MP]	C6[P]:[E][2P]
C7	Magnetism	C7,[P];[MP]	C7[P]:[E]

Contd...

	Basic Subject	Facet Formula	
		Ed 7 (1971)	Ed 6 (1960)
C9B3	Nuclear Physics	C9B3,[P];[MP]	C9B3[P]:[E][2P]
E	Chemistry	E,[P];[MP]	E[P]:[E][2P]
G	Biology	G,[P];[MP]	G[P]:[E][2P]
H1	Mineralogy	H1,[P];[MP]:[E]	H1[P]:[E][2P]
H2	Petrology	H2,[P];[MP]:[E]	H2[P]:[E][2P]
H7	Economic Geology	H7,[P];[MP]:[E]	H7[P]:[E][2P]
HX	Mining	HX,[P];[MP]	HZ[P],[P2]:[E][2P]
I	Botany	I,[P], [P2]; [MP]:[E]	I[P],[P2]:[E][2P]:[2E]
J	Agriculture	J[P],[P2]; MP]:[E],[2P]	J[P]:[E][2P];[2E]
K	Zoology	K,[P], [P2]; [MP]:[E]	K[P],[P2]:[E][2P]
KX	Animal Husbandry	KX,[P],[P2];[MP]:[E],[2P]	KZ[P]:[E][2P]:[2E][3P]
L	Medicine	L,[P], [P2]; [MP]:[E]	L[P]:[E][2P]:[2E][3P]
LX3	Pharmacology	LX3,[P];[MP]	LZ3[P]:[E][2P]
LX5	Pharmacopeia	LX5, [P]	LZ5[P],[P2]
M7	Textiles	M7,[P]; [MM]:[E]	M7[P]:[M]:[E][2P]
MJ7	Rope Making	MJ7,[P]; [MM]:[E]	MJ7[P]:[E][2P]
Δ	Spiritual Experience and Mysticism	Δ,[P],[P2];[MP]	Δ[P],[P2]:[E][2P]
NA	Architecture	NA,[P],[P2];[MP]	NA[P],[P2][P3],[P4]:[E]
NB	Town Planning	NB,[P],[P2];[MP]	NB[P],[P2][P3],[P4]:[E]
ND	Sculpture	ND,[P];[MM]: [E]	ND[P],[P2][P3];[M]:[E][2P]
NQ	Painting	NQ,[P];[MM]: [E]	NQ[P][P2][P3];[M]:[E][2P]
NR	Music	NR,[P];[MM]: [E]	NR[P],[P2][P3];[M]
O	Literature	O, [P],[P2],[P3];[P4]	O[P][P2][P3],[P4]
P	Linguistics	P,[P]. [P2]; [MP]	P[P],[P2][P3]:[E][2P]
Q	Religion	Q, [P]; [MP]	Q[P]:[E][2P]
R3	Metaphysics	R3, [P]	R3[P],[P2]
R4	Ethics	R4, [P], [P2]	R4[P],[P2]
S	Psychology	S, [P]; [MP]	S[P]:[E][2P]
T	Education	T,[P];[MP]	T[P]:[E][2P],[2P2]
V	History	V,[P],[P2];[MP]	V[P],[P2]:[E][2P]
W	Political Science	W,[P],[P2]:[MP]	W[P],[P2]:[E][2P]
Y	Sociology	Y,[P];[MP]:[E],[2P]	Y[P]:[E][2P]:[2E][3P]
Z	Law	Z,[P],[P2],[P3],[P4].	Z[P],[P2],[P3],[P4]

20

Fundamentals of Library Classification (B.I. Palmer's View)

Classification

Librarian is a Host.

Readers are Guests.

There are principles of orderly arrangement to reduce the cumulative loss of time to successive readers.

20.1 Traditional Grouping

Colour group → More colour group

Size group   → More size group

Author group → More author group → Individual group

Author group is more potent. The authorship, however, implies other qualities than merely who wrote it.

Example: Mathematician — to deal with maths.

Radio Engineer — to deal with wireless.

Greater potentiality leads to smaller group. If a reader looks for an author's work, he will look on a special subject. For more details he will consult bibliographies.

Author arrangement can only properly respond to an author approach to books. The title of the book is much less stable than its author's name. The title often conveys the subject contents of a book, indeed the title of the monograph or periodical article on a science or technical subject is usually a statement of a subject; but in the sciences where this is most common, title arrangement would result in there being quantities of items under the headings "Study", "Examination", "Analytical", etc. since title arrangement is arrangement by the accident of the first word. This method has the least claim of the three of the considerations.

1. **Subject arrangement:** Subject arrangement breaks down the collection into many small groups, provided the reader has a general idea of a subject with which his author was occupied in the book he is seeking. The task of picking it out from the small number of other books on the same subject is not an impossible one.

    Subject – means specific subject.

    Subject arrangement is a helpful arrangement by treating each subject separately.

2. **Helpful arrangement:** The order which displays subjects in such a way that a person approaching a group of subjects at any point is led by the order itself to the specific subject, and needs the following :

    (a) related material;

    (b) specific subjects that are only to be found with material of a more general nature;

    (c) specificity in the relative matter;

    (d) a fixed order, giving increasing specificity.

Order

General work first → followed by work on general subject treated specially → (than by) works on special subjects treated generally, → (and lastly by) works on special subject treated specially.

(i) The general treated generally –

    e.g. An Outline of **Medicine**

(ii) The general treated specially

    e.g. Surgery: a Manual.

(iii) Special treated generally

    e.g. **Stomach**: a Handbook.

(iv) Special treated specially

e.g. **Surgery of the Stomach.**

Arrangement of books demands that we give names of the groups into which we divide them, so that we can refer them conveniently.

The names thus given are called the terms of the classification.

1. Labelling the subject – MASONRY, CARPENTRY, TILING, PLANNING, PLASTERING

2. Choice of characteristics

Building
Planning
Masonry
Tiling
Carpentry
Plastering
Glazing

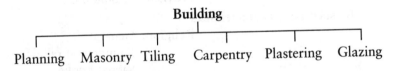

3. Coordinate groups –

Array = A. Canonical
B. Evolutionary
C. Spatial contiguity
D. Chronological
E. Alphabetical
F. Increasing complexity
G. Categorical

Facet

Every subject has one or more aspects which correlate to the characteristics used as a basis for division. We call sum the total of the divisions of each aspect as facet.

e.g. History of England — Chronological facet

Chronological facet always follows the geographical facet in the class number.

History	Geographical Facet	Chronological Facet
9	42 England	05 Tudor period

This division is called Facet analysis.

Foci: Every part of the facet is foci or major to minor divisions of a facet of any subject.

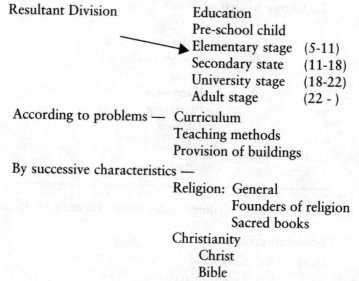

The process of division

Resultant Division   Education
                                  Pre-school child

Elementary stage (5-11)
Secondary state (11-18)
University stage (18-22)
Adult stage (22 -)

According to problems — Curriculum
                              Teaching methods
                              Provision of buildings

By successive characteristics —
                          Religion: General
                                      Founders of religion
                                        Sacred books
                        Christianity
                              Christ
                              Bible

Example: 1

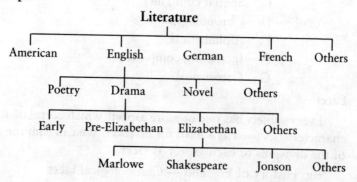

Example: 2

Literature

Array 2.	Literature	Literature	Literature
	English	English	English
	Poetry	Drama	Novel
Array 3.	Literature	Literature	Literature
	English	English	English
	Drama	Drama	Drama
	Early	Pre-Elizabethan	Elizabethan
Array 4.	Literature	Literature	Literature
	English	English	English
	Drama	Drama	Drama
	Elizabethan	Elizabethan	Elizabethan
	Marlowe	Shakespeare	Jonson

21

Classification (View of J.S. Mill)

21.1 What is Classification

Class + Fication = The process of division

We may call it divisionisation

Class means division

Fication means process.

Classification is based on thinking (Idea) – while we observe anything, we memorise it, keep in mind –

(a) What is knowledge?

(b) What is group of knowledge?

(c) What is homogeneous groups?

(d) How they have likeness or unlikeness with the subjects?

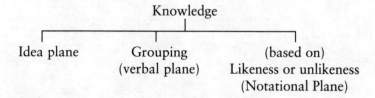

The word Classification is derived from Latin word "Classic".

It was first used in Ancient Rome to divide the group of persons (Rich and Poor, Master and Slaves).

This grouping was done on the basis of social structure.

Similarly in a library—the basic concept is "knower and knowee".

Knower: The person who seeks knowledge.
(Knowledge of entity)
Knower is called knowledge of entities and specific characteristics of knowledge.

Knower is a man as he has:

(a) A mind (understanding, expression).

(b) Thinking (perceives the knowledge and applies his mind).

(c) Extension of thinking (retrieves the thoughts).

21.2 When Knowledge Established

When knower knows something or has knowledge of something, knowledge is established—knower observes, applies senses and establishes the knowledge.

Knowledge is established because—

(a) Man has long life and lives for long period.

(b) A man lives upto three generations of this family. It means knowledge is preserved upto 3 generations. It is a continuous process.

(c) Man has understanding and reasoning and analyses his knowledge. It result into stock of knowledge. Hence, knowledge is extended.

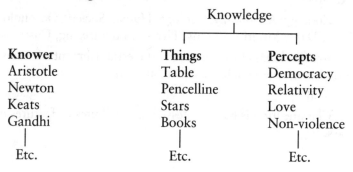

	Knowledge	
Knower	**Things**	**Percepts**
Aristotle	Table	Democracy
Newton	Pencelline	Relativity
Keats	Stars	Love
Gandhi	Books	Non-violence
Etc.	Etc.	Etc.

21.3 Division of Classification

Classification may be divided into two types:

1. **Natural Classification:** We call it a division by nature. It is made according to:

    (a) Natural plan.

    (b) Natural order.

    (c) Based on objectives.

    (d) Done for general purpose.

Natural classification is a division by nature. It is in idea plane.

Example: Earth, sky, stars, animals, man, sea, day, night, plants, fire, instruments, relatives, etc. are thought-based knowledge.

2. **Artificial Classification:** It is also known as constructive classification. It is a classification based on verbal and notational plane. When idea plane (knowledge) is transformed to verbal plane (terms) and terms are coded on the basis of notations (signs & symbols). It has the following advantages :

    (a) It is purposeful.

    (b) It is constructive.

    (c) It is specific.

    (d) It is meaningful.

    (e) It is in decoding form (coding when goes reverse in extension, it becomes decoding).

Example:

Zoology, Astronomy, Geology, Human Society, Oceonology, Time, Days, Months, Botany, Physics, Engineering, Customs.

Artificial classification means the establishment of terms in verbal language which are called subjects.

J.S. Mill

Classification is based on essential attributes or features of a class.

Mill has given a pyramid structure:

J.S. Mill's Pyramid Structure

OBJECT
(Every class or group of class has been determined
on the basis of objectives of study by man)

Common Features	Essential Features
(Every class has some common features applied in more than one class)	(Every class has individual or special features/character-istics, attributes which are not common to more than one class)

In series of entities
(All common features are put
in a sequence on the basis of
their common sequence)

In series of entities
(All specific features for
entities are put in a sequence
related to each other)

More general or less general or from greater extension to less extension
(The sequence of entities is again subdivied to such divisions)
(Greater extension to less extension means general to specific but like
entities in one group and unlike entities in other group)

Hence— Classification is inductive. Division is deductive.

21.4 Documents—Reading Material

Documents means the written record of information in the form of a book or non-book material and fit for handling.

1. It is a written or recorded document (physical form).

2. It can be transported.

3. It can be preserved.

4. Which is embodied.

5. Which has macro- and micro-thoughts.

6. Which fulfils the object of the reader.

7. Which may be transferable.

8. Which may be translated.

Example: Books, periodicals, maps, sound records, microfilm, cassettes, floppies, CDs, etc.

Each book

It contains individual knowledge,

It has knowledge of one entity.

These may be known as division's of knowledge.

Attributes

There are three attributes of classification requisites:

1. Knowledge.

2. Documents.

3. Classification.

21.5 Subject Approach

Documents are the reading sources of readers in a library. Whatever subject or class in established, it is based on the choice or approach of the readers. Subject approach may be common or minute, specific more extension, more specific, more minute knowledge and thus more helpful to researches. Every document is full of knowledge and represents class or subject, though it may be multifocal, multidimensional. It is basic knowledge of one subject, e.g. Chemical Physics may have basic knowledge of physics related to chemicals.

21.6 Reader's Approach

Every document has its own importance. It gives knowledge. It works as entity of knowledge. As it is written by human being, it inherits thoughts of specific field. Reader's common demand is a piece of knowledge, specific subject with a particular angle of thought.

22

Call Numbers Used in Libraries of USA and Library Uses of Congress Classification

Each book in a library has a unique call number. A call number is like on address: it tells us where the book is located in the library.

Call numbers appear on the spines of books and in the online catalog.

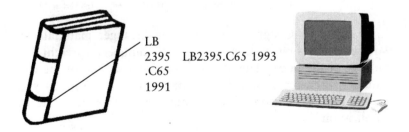

LB
2395   LB2395.C65 1993
.C65
1991

Note that the same call number can be written from top-to-bottom, or left-to-right.

Reading Call Numbers

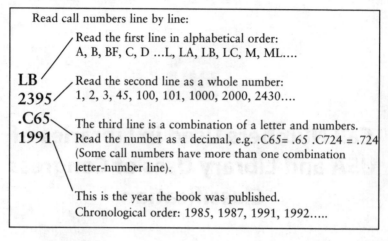

Read call numbers line by line:

> Read the first line in alphabetical order:
> A, B, BF, C, D ...L, LA, LB, LC, M, ML....

LB

> Read the second line as a whole number:
> 1, 2, 3, 45, 100, 101, 1000, 2000, 2430....

2395

.C65

1991

> The third line is a combination of a letter and numbers.
> Read the number as a decimal, e.g. .C65= .65 .C724 = .724
> (Some call numbers have more than one combination
> letter-number line).

> This is the year the book was published.
> Chronological order: 1985, 1987, 1991, 1992.....

22.1 Shelf Arrangement

To understand how call numbers are put in order in Library of Congress Classification, again look at each section of the call number.

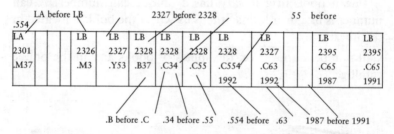

Library of Congress Classification arranges materials by subjects. The first sections of the call number represent the subject of the book. The letter-and-decimal section of the call number often represents the author's last name. And, as you recall, the last section of a call number is often the date of publication.

Example

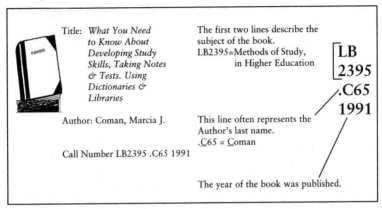

Title: *What You Need to Know About Developing Study Skills, Taking Notes & Tests. Using Dictionaries & Libraries*

The first two lines describe the subject of the book.
LB2395=Methods of Study, in Higher Education

Author: Coman, Marcia J.

This line often represents the Author's last name.
.C65 = Coman

Call Number LB2395 .C65 1991

The year of the book was published.

LB
2395
.C65
1991

This is important because books are classified by subject; you can often find several helpful books on the same shelf, or nearby. For example, within the same call number LB2395, there are other guides for college study.

LB	LB	LB	LB
2395	2395	2395	2395
.C6	.C65	1447	.O54
1960	1991		1983

A Successful Student's Handbook by Rita Phips

Key to College Success by Minnette Lenier

A Student's Guide to Efficient Study by Luella Cole

22.2 Location Prefixes – "LOCN"

When a call number looks like the examples above, (e.g. LB2395 .C65 1991), the book is shelved on the second floor of HCC Library. Some call numbers, however, are preceded by a location prefix.

Example:

Ref AG243 .G87 1992

The Ref prefix indicates that this book is shelved in the Reference Collection.

Location prefixes mean that book is shelved in a special place, and may have loan restrictions. Libraries uses the following location prefixes:

Prefix	Collection	HCC Library Location	Loan Period
[Blank]	Circulating Collection	2nd floor	28-day loan
Oversz	Oversize – a big book!	2nd floor, Diamond Head Wall	28-day loan
Ref	Reference Collection	1st floor	Library-use only
HawPac	Hawaii/Pacific Collection	2nd floor, Diamond Head Wall	14-day loan
HawPac Ref	Hawaii/Pacific Reference	1st floor, Diamond Head Side	Library-use only
Tech Ref	Automobile Technical Collection	1st Floor, Ewa side	Library-use only
Reserv	Reserve Book set aside for a class	1st floor, Circulation Counter	Set by instructor
Tele	Telecourse videotape	1st floor, Circulation Counter	Overnight

23

Citation Indexing

The traditional indexing systems suffer from a number of serious limitations.

More important among these are:

(a) Notation or subject headings are not always perfect. Sometimes, they are ambiguous having together different meanings, bringing in the problem of semantics and vocabulary control.

(b) Subject are growing at a fast rate. It is difficult for the subject labels to keep pace with this very fast growth.

(c) Traditional indexing is subject oriented and has limited utility in supporting multidisciplinary research, which is a present day phenomenon.

(d) Users take time to accept subject label.

(e) The tremendous growth of literature and the availability of limited number of indexes result into a serious time log.

(f) Indexers too have different capabilities. The same document may be indexed differently by different indexers.

To rename the above problems, it needs a better indexing system. The citation indexing system has been introduced to solve the problems of traditional indexes. It is based on the following two assumptions:

(a) A document giving citations of the previously published document indicates subject relationship between the current document and the old document; and

(b) The documents which cite the same publication have some subject relationship with each other.

The Institute for scientific information, Philadelphia, USA (ISO) has developed the citation index system.

Researchers in science and technology have traditionally supported their current articles with reference citations to previously published articles:

(a) To affirm or refute an argument or thesis.

(b) To clarify.

(c) To refer to a method or procedure.

(d) To credit or criticise a previous researcher.

(e) To indicate alternative directions.

(f) To provide a general frame of reference for their own research.

So important to good research articles has this practice become necessary that scientists can determine much about the subject content of a new article by examining its reference citation to earlier articles.

In traditional subject indexing, an inverted file of all the documents is constructed on the basis of a subject term. But a citation index takes a citation from a document and constructs an inverted file of all documents that cite the same reference. A citation index is a list of all works that have been cited in a particular year, and underneath each cited item are arranged the papers that have all cited the same original work.

The premise behind such technique is that the two papers citing the same paper have some subject relationship. This technique overcomes the problem of semantics and vocabulary control because dependence on subject term is not there.

Through citation indexing it is possible to approach a subject through the author or title by linking the two and taking them as chains in subject linkage. In fact, it treats the author as a subject and builds a chain that is unending.

23.1 History Citation Indexing

Citation Indexing originated in the "United States of America."

Frank Shepard's Citation index was the first pioneering effort which applied this technique in 1973.

Since in law a precedent is always considered relevant for future judgements, it is fruitful for a lawyer to base his arguments on previous judgements on a similar point of law. In USA, the Shepard's citations meet this need by displaying cited cases along with all those cases in which a cited case has been cited.

1952 — The Welch project concerned with indexing of medical literature and applied the Shepard's techniques to the indexing of scientific literature.

—   Eugene Carfield, a project investigator there, contributed a number of articles on the citation indexing and its application to the scientific literature.

—   The first science citation index was brought out as an experimental project in 1961.

—   Since 1965, SCI has been a regular publication.

—   Generic citation index was first brought out first in 1963.

1959 — The cumulative index to the *Journal of the American Statistical Association*, Vol. 35-50 was brought out. It has used the principles of citation indexing.

There are three more popular citation indexes:

(i) Shepard's Citation Index.

(ii) Science Citation Index.

(iii) Social Science Citation Index.

23.2 Scope and Coverage of Science Citation Index

(a) Science citation index is based entirely on the citations made in current documents.

(b) Except subject area.

(c) Coverage in terms of types of documents.

(d) Periodicals and inclusion of items—

    (i) Scanning

    (ii) Frequency of publication

    (iii) Format

    (iv) Method of presentation

    (v) Nature of the supporting indexes.

These decisions determine the nature and individual characteristic of each indexing service.

Subject Coverage: 700 periodicals as source material it includes articles, short communications, letters etc. but also abstracts , reviews, corrections and errata, discussions, conference items, editorials, tributes, arbitraries etc.

— Only those items which do not have any citations in them will be automatically excluded.

— The frequency of the SCI is quarterly.

— The last issue in December.

— Cumulative issue for the whole year. Science citation index started with three parts—

    (i) Citation index.

    (ii) Source index.

    (iii) Permuterm subject index (From 1966)

        each part has a—

        (a) Different structure.

        (b) Contains different types of information.

23.3 Citation Index Part

(a) It presents the current literature of the source journals, under an ordered listing of the cited documents.

(b) The cited documents are arranged alphabetically by the name of the respective first author.

(c) One cited reference is followed by the next cited reference.

(d) Each cited reference is represented by the—

    (i) Name of the first author

    (ii) Year

   (iii) Title of the document or journal

   (iv) Volume number

    (v) Starting page number.

(e) File of the citing document is not available unless it is monographic publication. Thus, if an article in a source journal has cited ten references then the same article will be featured under each of these ten references in citation index.

(f) Anonymous cited document, i.e. items where no personal authorship is attributed, are arranged separately, alphabetically by the titles of publications.

(g) Cited patents are arranged separately in numerical order of the patent numbers. This section within the citation index is named patent citation index.

In other words, cited index part is a list of cited items arranged alphabetically by their authors. Under each cited item is displayed a list of citing items arranged again alphabetically by their authors. If there are more than one cited items or citing items by the same author, these are arranged chronologically. Each cited item displays the name of the first author, year of publication, journal where published, its volume number and the first page number of the item, all given in an abbreviated form.

Similarly, a citing item carries information about author and bibliographic details of the citing document such as, title, nature, volume, first page and year of publication. The nature of the citing document such as:

    (i) Title

   (ii) Nature — indicated by coded symbols as A, C, D, E, I, L, M, N

   (iii) Volume

   (iv) First page

    (v) Year of publication.

Nature: The nature of the citing document is indicated by such coded symbols as A, C, D, E, I, L, M, N, which respectively represent:

(a) Abstract

(b) Corrections

(c) Discussions

(d) Editorials

(e) Tributes

(f) Obituaries

(g) Letters

(h) Proceedings of meetings

(i) Technical notes.

Example: 1— Citation Index of Science Citation Index

NICHOLS   WH

68	JCHEM PHY	49	1000	
BOON JP	PHYSREVA	2	2542	70
CANDAU	ANN PHYSIQ	4	21	69
CARDMON MJ	J OPT SOCL	60	1264	70

Letter

The cited item is authorised by W.H. Nichols and has appeared in 1968 in the *Journal of Chemical Physics* in its Volume 49 at pages 1000 onwards.

The first document citing this item is authorised by J.P. Boon published in the *Physics Review A* in its Volume 2 at page 2542 in year 1970. The letter L in the third citing item indicates that it is a letter.

Example: 2

Cited	Author	Publication	Citing Yr	Vol.	Page
UREY HC	31	PHY REV	——	38	1969
PILLAI MGK	(1931)	AUSTJ CHEM	65	42	952
TADOCORO H		J CHEM PHYS	65	42	1432
————	62	SCIENCE	——	137	623
MUELLER G		NATURE	L65	205	1200

Letter

A paper by H.C. Urey published in the year 1931 in the journal *Physical Reviews*, Volume 38, page 1969 has been cited in two current 1965 papers by M.G.K. Pillai and H. Tadokoro and their respective bibliographical details are also given.

The dotted line indicates that another paper by the same author, i.e. U.C. Urey , has also been cited by G. Mueller. The document code L indicates that the citing item is a letter (to the editor). The double asterisks with the cited year 31 (i.e. 1931) is an indication that this is the first or starting cited entry by the particular author.

23.4 Source Index

The source index is a part of Science Citation Index contains additional bibliographic information about the current citing articles included in the citation Index part. It is, in fact, a complete author index of all items in source periodicals included in the Science Citation Index during a particular period.

(a) The arrangement is alphabetical by the first citing author.

(b) All the co-authors are cross–referred to the first author.

(c) For corporate works, there exists a separate section in the source index. These works are arranged there alphabetically by the names of the organisations where the work was done.

(d) Besides the citing author and his collaborators, the other bibliographical details provided by the source index are:

  (i) The title of the source periodicals

  (ii) Its volume

  (iii) Page

  (iv) Year of publication

  (v) No. of references it has

  (vi) Issue number of the source periodical.

Example: One Source Index of Science Citation Index

BOON JP (Author and co-author)
DEGUENT P –

PHYS	REV	A 2	2542	70	36R	N6
		(vol.)	(page)	(pub. yr.)	(no. of ref.)	(issue no.)

TRANSPORT FUNCTIONS AND LIGHT SCATTERED IN SIMPLE DENSE FLUIDS (Full title)

Two Source Index of SCI

BROOKS BC

J DOC	24	41	65	12R	48284

MEASUREMENT OF INFORMATION RETRIEVAL EFFECTIVENESS PROPOSED BY SWEAT

BROWN HL   JAMES T

AM DOC	19	30	66	10R

EVALUATION OF DOCUMENT SEARCHING SYSTEMS

COOPER WS		LIB	ASSOC			(Gr. Brit.)
	J DOC	29	22	68	L	6R
	EXPECTED	SEARCH LENGTH				
JAMES T		SEE BROWN HL				

J.P. Boon in collaboration with P. Degrent published a paper entitled as "Transport functions and light scattering in sample dense fluids" in the *Physics Review A* in 1970 which appeared in Volume 2, No. 6 at page 2542. The paper has 36 references.

The display shows that H.L. Brown and T. James have published a paper entitled 'Evaluation of Document Searching Systems'. This paper has been published in Volume 19 of the *American Documentation* during 1966 at page 30 onwards. The paper has 10 references. T. James, the co-author, has also been shown as cross-referenced to H.L. Brown in the last line.

Example:

Corporate Index part in Source Index of Science Citation Index

LIBRARY ASSOCIATION (GT BRITAIN) [Organisation attributed]

COOPER WS	JDOC	68	2	29	22
(Citing author)	(journal)	(year)	(volume)		(page)

SOURCE INDEX PART

MUELLER DC	INT	BUS	MARCH	
3165719 US		65	P 2R	JAN 12
MUELLER EG 'SEE'		SMITH	HL 3166263 US	
MUELLER G	CLAUS G	SUBAC	EA	
NATURE	205	1200 65	L	10R
NG97762558				

INTERPRETATION OF MICRO-STRUCTURES IN CARBONACEOUS
METEORITES

It shows that G. Muller, with the collaboration of G. Claus and E.A. Subac published a letter in the nature in 1965 which appeared in page 1200 of volume 205, number 4977. The full title of this communication is also given in the next line. It is further shown that it contains ten references and its accession number in the ISI collection is 62558.

Search Strategy

(a) The use of Science Citation Index is simple.

(b) No artificial languages or special nomenclatures are involved.

In searching, a searcher begins his search with an earlier published item (article, book, letter etc.) which he knows is related to his subject. He looks up the citation of this item utilising the name of the author from the Citation Index portion of Science Citation Index. There he finds all current articles that have referred to the Cited earlier article. Complete bibliographical details of the citing documents can be had from the source Index. This helps the user to find the relevance of these citing documents to his query.

This search may be further expanded to build a more extensive bibliography to the subject of query, other papers of the citing authors can serve as many entry point to the Citation

Index and Science Citation Index. This process which is called 'cycling' can be continued to build up a comprehensive bibliography on a particular subject. 'Cycling' yields good results because authors do write more than one paper on the same subject as also usually in the field of specialisation.

Merits of Citation Index (Advantages)

(a) No intellectual activity is involved in the compilation of a Citation Index.

(b) Its compilation is mechanical and it uses in-built relations of citing and cited documents.

(c) It enables the prompt publication of this index reducing the time lag between the reporting of information in the primary journals and its inclusion in the Citation Index considerably.

(d) Citation Index is free from terminology problems. It is not effected by the changing terminology or by the new concepts.

(e) A document in the citation Index is represented by its author, title, journal etc. and this presentation is permanent.

Most of the indexing systems use cross references to link a subject with related subjects for permitting comprehensive search to the users.

(f) Searching of relevant materials can be done more easily and speedily in the citation index than in other conventional indexes.

(g) The citation index presents each time a different pattern of the past literature when viewed in different points in time.

(h) Citation index helps in finding out case (high standard) periodicals in the subject.

(i) Citation index reveals the obsolescence of the published material.

(j) Citation index may reveal the genesis of a newly emerging subject.

(k) Reading material is available in various physical forms.

(l) Citation index also reveals main scientists or researchers in a particular field as also their scientific activities.

(m) Any scientist may like to see whether his contribution has been appreciated, applied or criticised by the other scientists. A citation index gives this information also. In the light of this feedback, a scientist can pursue his work further.

Limitations

(a) A citation index does not provide logical subject arrangement which is helpful to the users.

(b) A citation index does not specify the nature of relationship cited document has with the citing documents.

(c) All documents are not consulted by the author. Cited by him in his work, so highly relevant document might be missed, without them citation index remain incomplete.

(d) Citation Index retrieves related documents only and not the contents of the documents.

(e) Citation index does not satisfy the exhaustive approach of the user.

Conclusion

(i) The success of citation index is dependent on the efficiency of citation practice of authors.

(ii) SCI has solved most of the problems inherent among conventional indexes.

(iii) There is no terminology problem.

(iv) Its multi-disciplinary coverage, convenience and speed are other advantages.

Index